The Good Soil

The Good Soil

Reclaiming the Lost Art of Discipleship

Allen C. Hughes

Foreword by Leith Anderson

RESOURCE *Publications* · Eugene, Oregon

THE GOOD SOIL
Reclaiming the Lost Art of Discipleship

Resource Publications
An Imprint of Wipf and Stock Publishers
199 W. 8th Ave., Suite 3
Eugene, OR 97401

www.wipfandstock.com

PAPERBACK ISBN: 978-1-7252-9541-4
HARDCOVER ISBN: 978-1-7252-9540-7
EBOOK ISBN: 978-1-7252-9542-1

03/15/21

Contents

Acknowledgements

I WANT TO THANK my wife Louise and my four boys, Chaplin, James, Josh and Dargan for their love and support. Thanks as well to Terry Walling, my mentor and coach, and to all those who edited this book, especially Jody Godby and Jason Radcliff. Thanks also to The Anglican Mission in America (AMiA), the organization I work for, who graciously allowed me to develop these ideas both on paper and in practice. Last but certainly not least, thanks to the intercessory team who faithfully prayed me through the tough times.

Foreword

WHAT IS MOST IMPORTANT for every soldier in every army? The ancient answer is not pay, equipment, training, victory or survival. The top answer is attributed to experts from the Roman general Julius Caesar to the "father of modern management" Peter Drucker 2000 years later. They said that "the soldier has a right to competent command."

History is strewn with examples from the worst to the best—incompetent officers who betrayed their troops to competent commanders who did well. At both extremes and in between have been soldiers who followed leaders with the hope that they were trustworthy and that their commands were right.

As disciples of Jesus Christ we commit to the command of our Savior and Lord. All of our lives are on the line; even our eternal destinies. Like soldiers in regular armies we often are called to believe in strategies and obey orders that we can't fully understand—all from a top leader we can't see in person.

Our discipleship is built on the biblical promise that Jesus will *always* provide competent command. We may not always have the highest pay, best equipment, complete training nor exemption from suffering or death. What we will always have is our Lord who is all-knowing, all-wise, omni-competent and loves us beyond our understanding. While military officers are sometimes good and sometimes not, none of them are perfect. Only Jesus is the perfect commander who we can totally trust in every battle and circumstance. Being a disciple of Jesus is the smartest, wisest and best choice we can make.

The next big question is how are we to think and act as disciples of our competent Lord. It's a question that has thousands of correct answers. Many answers are in the Bible from the words of Jesus to the reports of fellow followers. But, answers vary by each disciple's age, generation and situation. Just as soldiers follow orders differently when given desk duty in logistics at headquarters than when on the battlefield in hand-to-hand combat, so do we follow Jesus differently as healthy college athletes and as weakened cancer survivors.

Turn the coming pages and hear the questions, experiences and counsel of a fellow disciple of Jesus who tells about following Jesus in chapters of calling, equipping, community and ministry. Learn and live out discipleship that is personalized to you. Just remember that we are loyally committed to the amazingly and consistently competent Jesus. Let us be like those first disciples who heard Jesus say "Come, follow me." "At once they left their nets and followed him." (Matthew 4:19–20)

Leith Anderson

1

The Good Soil

WHETHER MY LOVE OF gardening sprang from seeing the fruits of my own labor or grew out of the connection created with my dad from laboring side by side, I do not know. I remember vividly planting tomato seeds as a young boy with my father. Although I have never liked tomatoes, the outdoors felt like home to me and time with my father like a gift from heaven itself. So each day, I was drawn to the garden like a child to the family room on Christmas morning. To my astonishment after burying tiny seeds in the earth, I found small sprouts that had burst forth seemingly overnight. Fascinated, I diligently monitored their progress from sprouts to long leafy plants with branches weighed down by luscious, red, homegrown tomatoes. My father and I together had labored, waited, and witnessed a miracle—life from a tiny seed. I was hooked and have been gardening ever since.

Years of gardening have taught me that there are great mysteries at work, things beyond my control—God is at work in His creation. Although God could do as He wished without our help or the passage of time, He has reserved a place for us in His plan. Even before the fall, Adam and Eve were given work. They were charged with tending the Garden; and, growth cannot be taken for granted. Growth requires effort. We co-labor with God.

As a boy, I thought all that was necessary was to plant the seeds and then sit back and watch the garden grow. As I grew older, I recognized the hard work required to create the good soil that would produce a bountiful harvest. I needed to fertilize, weed, watch for pests, and rotate crops to enable the garden to produce to its fullest potential.

Good soil is essential to a healthy, thriving garden. Good soil contains critical minerals and trace elements that plants need for life and health. Good soil retains water that is the lifeblood of plants. Good soil underneath makes possible the fruit in plain sight. But, creating good soil requires time and effort.

Scripture uses numerous gardening analogies to illustrate principles of discipleship. Discipleship is the lifelong pursuit of learning to live under the guidance and care of our Father. Discipleship requires time and effort; and, cultivating the habits of discipleship creates fertile soil for growth in the image of God and the abundant life.

> According to Strong's Concordance, the Greek word for disciple is *mathētēs*.[1] HELPS Word-studies gives this further explanation:[2] "mathētēs . . . the "*mental effort* needed to think something through")—properly, a learner; a disciple, a follower of Christ who learns the doctrines of Scripture and the lifestyle they require; someone catechized with proper instruction from the Bible with its necessary follow-through (life-applications).

Christian discipleship is the lifelong process of learning from Jesus. A disciple is someone who continuously looks to Christ for teaching, leading, instruction, correction, and love. Diligent practice of discipleship yields the fruits of the good soil—unconditional love, joy, and peace regardless of circumstances, and meaningful work.

In the church today, there is a growing desire to return to the heart of discipleship. As believers, most of us set out with an earnest desire to be fully committed disciples, but we become distracted or stuck. To further complicate matters, the word "discipleship" in our culture has been misunderstood, misapplied, reduced in scope, and in some cases used to manipulate serious, faithful Christians.

The result is that many live with an anemic understanding of discipleship which inhibits growth and maturity, causes vocational confusion, and keeps believers on the periphery of the full Christian life. When we earnestly and fully engage in discipleship, we understand our identity as sons or daughters of the Living God. We are able to discern our calling in advancing His Kingdom on earth and are aware of the natural and spiritual gifts He has given us. We know His voice and have direction. We persevere

1. (https://biblehub.com/greek/3101.htm).
2. Helps Word-studies: Copyright © 1987, 2011 by Helps Ministries, Inc.

through challenges and hardship; and, we experience His pleasure in us and His power at work in us.

As a minister working with hundreds of churches across multiple denominations, I have encountered men and women everywhere who want to be engaged in serious discipleship. Nevertheless, many who have been Christians for decades report feeling like they do not live a life that attracts non-believers to the faith. Unable to gain lasting victory over the sin patterns in their own lives or to confidently recognize the voice of God, they do not know what to do. They go to church on Sundays, and yet they are not experiencing the anticipated growth. Their experience of the Christian life does not measure up to the abundant life that Jesus promises. While they long for this growth and abundant life, many are embarrassed to admit that they do not fully understand the meaning of being a disciple of Jesus Christ. Many feel shame for not having figured this out already, and this shame hinders them from moving forward.

Conversely, many mistakenly believe they have a solid understanding of discipleship when, in reality, they lack an understanding of the complexity of discipleship—how it works and how all the pieces fit together. Unfortunately, because most have found a few tools and practices that have worked at some point, they keep using them despite the lack of sustained fruitfulness. We need help seeing the big picture.

As an early gardener, I wondered how complicated gardening could be. Surely gardening would come naturally, and I could figure out whatever I did not know as I went along. Frustrated and humbled after a few seasons of much work with little to no fruit, I needed help. I read books, watched gardening shows, asked questions of more experienced gardeners, and learned good practices. I learned which tools to use for which jobs and which products could address which problems. I habitually monitored the soil and learned to identify and eradicate pests. Shocked at the amount of learning necessary, I discovered that successful gardeners are always learning from others. Thankfully, I learned and matured as a gardener, and the result was good soil in which my plants grew, thrived, and produced fruit.

The Jewish culture of Jesus' day had a firm grasp of discipleship. There was no formal education like we have today. Preparation for becoming a judge or religious leader required study beginning at the age of thirteen as a *disciple* under a scholar or expert in the field. The Apostle Paul is an example of this practice. As a boy in the Jewish culture, Paul was sent from his home to study the Law under a highly regarded religious leader named

Gamaliel, a Rabbi in Jerusalem (Acts 5:34; 22:3). Paul's parents understood that if he were to become a religious leader, his discipleship would require much time and commitment. Effective discipleship involved more than the transfer of information. The process included imitating the teacher's life, absorbing his values, and reproducing his teachings. Proficiency required years of diligent study while abiding with the teacher.

Today many Christians approach discipleship with the same attitude I had as a novice gardener, just assuming that it would come naturally. This book is an attempt to correct that attitude in regard to discipleship. Throughout the book, I use the image Jesus used of "good soil" in speaking to the twelve disciples (Matthew 13). In this analogy, Jesus explains that the message of the Kingdom can fall on different kinds of soil, each yielding different results. Only good soil produces growth and bears good fruit.

Just as Jesus described the seed that fell on rocky or weed-infested soil, much of our discipling seed has been thwarted by barriers in our culture. We need to identify those and remove them from the soil. Then we need to survey that ground and consider the big picture.

Imagine creating a garden without the end product in mind. You will not know how to start; you will have an impossible time assessing progress; and, you will not be able to foresee problems. You will end up with a mess. We need the big picture clearly in mind before we proceed. For discipleship, this picture is comprised of these major foci:

- God's Calling on our lives
- How He continually Equips and trains us
- How He gives us a Community to help in this process
- And finally, how we each have a specific Ministry that God intends to bear much fruit.

For two reasons, I am not trying to cover each principle of discipleship exhaustively. First, I intend to present discipleship as the mysterious and multifaceted art that it is and move away from the rationalistic, controllable, and manageable process it has become. Secondly, entire books have been devoted to each of the ideas I highlight and have been written in a much more scholarly fashion while quoting serious theologians and other sources.

Once we get the big picture, we will focus on the daily, weekly, and yearly habits and rhythms that ensure the right conditions for growth. The habits and rhythms are the work of discipleship. As with the soil, God gives the growth in discipleship, but we also do the work.

ONGOING CYCLE OF DISCIPLESHIP

Calling
"Hearing God"

Community
"The Body of Christ"

Ministry
"The good works called to do"

Equipping
"Character and gifting"

At heart, I am a practitioner of the Christian faith with a longing to follow the call that God has for me. Consequently, for fellow practitioners who share that desire, I offer a fuller understanding of the breadth of discipleship components. We may have read the Bible, been to church, participated in activities, prayed, read Christian books, been in small groups, and gone on mission trips—all valid components in the life of a disciple. However, there is much more.

G. K. Chesterton reminds us in his book, *What's Wrong with the World,* that "the Christian ideal has not been tried and found wanting. It has been found difficult; and left untried."[3] This quote is an invitation and challenge to enter into the bountiful and multifaceted life of discipleship that God is offering you.

Of course, every gardener needs the proper tools, and every tool needs a proper context. Joy and satisfaction are the result of having the right tool for the job. That is true for discipleship also. I want us to understand the tools of discipleship and when they should and should not be used. I want

---

3. *What's Wrong with the World* (San Francisco, Ignatius Press, 1994), 1:37.

us to be able to discern the health of the soil and then to know which tool is appropriate to improve the soil.

Tools are the programs, events, classes, podcasts, and other teaching mediums we use to reap the harvest. Using and understanding tools are essential to discipleship. I want us to understand how the tools fit into the whole without getting too specific about the best tools for fear that the focus will be on the tools rather than on the fuller understanding of discipleship.

Throughout the book, there will be questions for reflection. My intent is that you will discern your place in the process of discipleship and identify the necessary steps that will bring you more fully into the abundant life God promises His disciples. So, I invite you to join me on this journey and hope it will leave you asking for more detail and specific examples.

Let me repeat that! I hope you will hunger for more depth and detail about how to incorporate the principles into your life and community. This book is attempting to bring those questions to the surface, not answer them. However, I have created a website with online discussions to supplement the book. These videos and podcasts will go deeper and be more specific by allowing you to hear from others who have processed these ideas. Links to the website are provided at the end of each chapter. You can find us at TheGoodSoil.us for deeper discussions of each of the topics discussed in the book.

Finally, I write this book because God loves us and desires to walk with us. God, our Father, sent His Son Jesus Christ not to condemn us but to save us and give us abundant life. He died on the cross so that our sin and brokenness would no longer keep us from Him. He invites us to be His followers, and He disciples us as we participate in His work on earth. His calling on our lives is the simple but hard work of learning to be His disciples so that others may know Him also. All I want to do is to give away everything that has been entrusted to me

2

Current Barriers to Discipleship

WHEN A PLANT IS weak and unfruitful, the gardener's first task is to diagnose the problem. What is preventing productive growth? Similarly, American Christians need to diagnose the problems and identify the barriers so that we can consider healthy behavior habits and rhythms that will move us towards growth as disciples. In Matthew 7:5, Jesus tells us that we should first remove the plank in our own eye before trying to help out our brother. In other words, if we start with healthy self-reflection, we can more effectively aid others. This chapter is an effort to help identify some of the planks in our "cultural Christian eyes" that need to be removed. In essence, if we really want to help others we must first understand and then address our problems.

The first step is admitting we have a problem. Recent Gallup Polls show a trend of growing unbelief in the American Church. In the last ten years, over 2 million more people say they "have no religious affiliation." In the last fifteen years over 4 million people have changed their minds from having a "great deal" or "quite a lot" of confidence in the church or organized religion to having "very little" or "no" confidence in the church or organized religion. 76% of Americans say religion is losing influence in our culture.[1]

In my twenties, I became an assistant coach for a college soccer team. I was a fairly good player and a prolific scorer, so the head coach put me in charge of coaching the guys in the shooting drills. I will never forget our

---

1. "Religion," IN DEPTH TOPICS A To Z, Gallup, November 28, 2016, http://www.gallup.com/poll/1690/religion.aspx Nov 28, 2016.

debrief after the first day of coaching. He bluntly said, "What were you doing out there? It certainly was not coaching. All you were doing was telling them to shoot the ball into the net—they already know that."

He explained to me that all my comments were simply encouragement to be better without explaining how. They knew what the outcome was supposed to be—to score. My job was to help them see why they were missing the target and specifically what they needed to change. Honestly, this took a while, but I finally realized that the key to helping them was to clearly identify what they were doing wrong.

I learned to recognize when they planted their non-dominant foot too close or too far away from the ball; I saw when they had their weight shifted too far back; I realized that many of them had the wrong head position when striking the ball. Once I understood the problem, I was able to craft drills to break the bad habits and develop habits and rhythms that would improve their shots.

We, as the American church, are shrinking. We cannot continue to keep doing what we have been doing in these past decades and expect anything but more decline. The sobering reality behind these statistics is not that we have spent less money, less time, or less thought on the church. On the contrary, we have spent more than ever. What we need is to restore a clear vision for discipleship.

As G. K. Chesterton reminds us, discipleship is hard, it is challenging, and we as the church have too often chosen an easier path. We must believe that if we become committed to true discipleship, we can change our culture. Consider this: If even 1% of American Christians were discipling one person a year who would then disciple one person *ad infinitum*, then all of the United States would be converted in less than a decade.

Certainly, it is simple to throw out statistics like this; however, I believe we must understand why we are in this constant decline in the church before we can make lasting change. What is it about our efforts to disciple others that have gone so wrong? If we ask any church in the country, we will probably be told that they have a plan for discipleship, that they are, in fact, trying to disciple the congregation. I have never talked to a church leader who did not say they were actively trying to disciple the congregation. Jesus described this phenomenon in the parable of the soils. He explained it like this:

> The seed falling on rocky ground refers to someone who hears the word and at once receives it with joy. But since they have no root, they last only a short time. When trouble or persecution comes

because of the word, they quickly fall away. The seed falling among the thorns refers to someone who hears the word, but the worries of this life and the deceitfulness of wealth choke the word, making it unfruitful. But the seed falling on good soil refers to someone who hears the word and understands it. This is the one who produces a crop, yielding a hundred, sixty, or thirty times what was sown. (Matthew 13:20–23)

Too often in our experience, the seed that is cast has not led to the "hundred, sixty or thirty times what was sown." Instead the worries of the world, our troubles, and the deceitfulness of wealth choke out the fruit we all desire.

As is often the case, the problem with our discipleship strategy is that it is dressed up in things that look like the real thing. Our efforts satisfy some general standards, and they bear some fruit; but, all too often, they are half measures. That is the real problem—someone who is only half-discipled is not truly discipled. More importantly, they do not feel equipped to disciple others. This is the sticking point. They have gone through the program, the class, or whatever has been "offered" and have come out the other side unequipped. They simply do not become disciples who will make other disciples.

It is not that we have not tried. It is not that the church did not have good intentions. Seed was cast, but somewhere along the way, we forgot that the fruit of our labor was intended to be exponential. Most Christians have tried some plan for discipleship and often have found some fruit in the process; however, whether they are unwilling or embarrassed to admit to needing more, they do not realize that it's the soil that needs amending.

So, what are the weeds and thorns and rocky soil that hinder our growth? What are some of the inherent flaws in many common discipleship "paths" employed in the Western church? Let's examine various key components of good soil that are missing and vital to discipleship.

UNHEALTHY DISCIPLESHIP PATHS

The Intellectual Path

Luke is a sixty-three-year-old physician. He has been in the church all of his life. He was a member of my church and would sign up for every class, every program, and every retreat. It was also clear to me that he had a gift for teaching. I approached him to ask if he would consider taking over and teaching my Sunday school class. He explained that he was not ready yet because there was so much more to learn. After forty years in the church, he still doubted his readiness. I wondered why after all the teaching he had received, he had not developed into a disciple who could disciple others.

Discipleship at its heart is about learning over a lifetime. We understand that there is a major intellectual component to our faith which, after all, is about learning a new way of life. We are to love God with all our mind. Our faith is about learning to live as we were intended to live before the Fall, learning to walk with the Father again, learning the habits that are good or bad for the soul.

The church, especially the Evangelical church, takes this part of discipleship seriously. We love to teach, to preach, and to tell others a better way to live. We try to get people to "learn their Bible." We try to get people to come to hear our sermon series, attend classes, and presumably participate in our programs so that they can learn and be discipled.

The church expects that as people learn, they will produce some fruit in their lives. The reasoning is that if they are learning they are being and becoming disciples; however, all too often, well-intentioned men and women armed with the best intellectual offerings of the church try to implement change in their lives with little to no lasting effect. Their intellect understands, but their behaviors remain unchanged. Or, too often they change for a while, but the change cannot be sustained.

In the wake of these results, the church reasons that we must teach more, teach more effectively, and go deeper intellectually. In short, we need to get more information into the heads of those we disciple because what we have put in their heads must not be enough. The underlying assumption is that we should expect transformation through information.

Moreover, we have cadres of well-informed Christians who believe they need to learn more before they can go out into the world and make disciples of others. I cannot tell you how many Christians I have met who have been in the church for ten years or more who still say they need more equipping before they are ready to disciple others.

Furthermore, when we make experts out of pastors, many Christians think we should leave discipleship to those experts; so, they never get into the game. Consequently, we have a cyclical, self-defeating mindset that fuels the need for more teaching in order to impart more information so that one day those in the church will finally be discipled enough to make a difference in their own lives and the lives of others.

Again, I am not implying that there is no value in teaching or in our intellectual pursuits and discussions. Rather, I am stating that when there is an over-emphasis on a purely rational understanding of the Christian faith and the biblical story, then discipleship becomes impotent. Often the components of the faith such as mystery, relationships, suffering, emotion, experience, and revelation, among others, are left out of the discipleship paths in the over-intellectual churches.

These churches often reject emotional or experiential modes of discipleship as a reaction to the over-emphasis and misuse of these modalities in other churches or settings. In our modern world, we have a high value and respect for information, education, and intellectual discourse. Consequently, the path of over-intellectualizing discipleship often goes unnoticed, and those who try to challenge or correct this trend are dismissed as non-intellectual and fatuous.

We live in a world where information is readily available. Access to the best books, teachings, and Bible studies are merely a click or two away. Moreover, getting information is inexpensive. Through the internet, almost anyone can access the best teachers in the world for very little money. The over-intellectualization path of discipleship claims that by incessantly learning more and more you will change. Unfortunately, this has never been the reality for man.

In Matthew 23, Jesus pointed out that many of the Jews and the religious leaders knew the commandments, but their hearts were like stone, and they failed to practice what they knew. Most Christians know they are supposed to love their brother as themselves yet struggle daily to make that a reality. The problem in proper discipleship is usually not a lack of information but rather an inability to address issues of the heart. Scripture reflects this truth with a powerful image: "We need the laws to be written on our hearts, not on tablets of stone" (Ezekiel 11:19).

When Jesus became man and walked with us, He confronted the established church and their tendency to over-intellectualize the faith. He addressed the Pharisees and teachers of the Law quoting scripture back to them from Isaiah: "'These people honor me with their lips, but their hearts are far from me. They worship me in vain; their teachings are merely human rules'" (Matthew 15:8–9).

Again, in Matthew 25, Jesus confronted the Pharisees and accused them of heaping the burden of their teachings on the backs of the people while not lifting a hand to teach them the joy and freedom of the faith. He was telling the Pharisees that they were not helping the people by their deep teachings, their articulate explanations of the Law, or their well thought out sermons. In fact, they were not helping them at all but were burdening them and preventing them from experiencing abundant life. Remember that the Pharisees were respected; they were the religious leaders; they were in charge of teaching the people; and, in the eyes of Jesus, they were an utter failure.

In the Old Testament, God promises us a Messiah who will change our hearts into hearts of flesh not hearts of stone. God knows that knowledge alone will not suffice. He clearly explains this, and yet, the religious leaders continued to ignore this truth. Even after our Savior has come, we live in a vicious cycle.

Christians go to church, and many earnestly desire to change. Unfortunately, too often they report being unable to make the desired behavioral changes. Then they seek more knowledge through sermons, classes, and Bible studies. Some even get into deep theology in hopes that this knowledge will unlock the door for them to be the disciples they desire to be. Nevertheless, they do not reap the true fruit they long for and grow increasingly frustrated with their faith, the church, and their efforts.

In addressing this conundrum, Thomas à Kempis stated, "There is no knowledge in this world that is not mixed with some ignorance. Therefore, a humble self-knowledge is a surer way to God than a search after deeper learning."[2]

He was not trying to dismiss the importance of deep learning. Rather, he was stressing the fact that mere information would not lead to transformation. He knew that what most Christians truly need is soul care. They need the caring and focused examination of the soul. Unfortunately, this cannot be sufficiently addressed in a classroom setting or by listening to a sermon or learning theology. There is a relational component.

Soul care must be done one-on-one, life on life. Jesus modeled this with His twelve disciples. He did not burden them with more knowledge, more laws, more how-to's, or more Bible studies. Rather He lived among them. He spent time with them and spoke individually into their lives.

The Corporate Program Path

When I was growing up, the common practice in our church and others was to reach the lost by mimicking corporate American culture. We wore

2. Thomas à Kempis, *The Imitation of Christ*, Book 1, Chapter 4.

the clothes they wore. We used the language they used and followed the models of organization and evaluation that had worked so successfully for businesses. We renamed our churches, redid the interiors, and built buildings with coffee shops.

Frankly, we had some success. We took down hurdles that were keeping people from coming to faith and spoke to them in a language they could understand. In short, we successfully rid the church of some archaic practices that were non-essential to the faith and had no meaning in the 21st century.

Unfortunately, in too many places and in too many ways, we threw out the proverbial baby with the bathwater and created a corporate path of discipleship. This path was the result of the church's good intentions to be effective and efficient. It is a very western, pragmatic, and systematic approach.

We worked hard to create simple and understandable paths to enable people to become disciples. We created programs like "the four bases," "the five shapes," and other diagrams and acrostics that were easy to remember. We then applied resources, energy, and the best marketing to attract as many people as possible into these programs with the hope that they would come out on the other side being discipled.

Again, these models have merit. Participation in these programs often leads to growth in faith; however, there is almost always a lingering sense that more is needed. The individual usually finishes the program with an unarticulated sense that they are not yet fully formed as a disciple. They wonder if they should run the bases again; if there is a higher-level program that would have the answers; or, if there is another church with better or deeper programs. They are left scratching their heads.

A common experience I have heard from Christians in this culture can be summed up as follows: "I go to church on Sunday and am part of a small group. I have been through the programs offered and I tithe. There is no indication that there is anything more I need to be doing as a Christian. Yet, I do not think I am growing as a disciple. I don't think I am going to run around the bases again. There has to be more!"

The truth is that there is more, and they know it. No matter how good the programs are or how efficiently they are run, the "corporate program" path fails to meet the criteria of discipleship. Most of our lives are spent at work, in our marriages, in parenting, in taking care of our homes and in relating to neighbors. That's where the chaos is experienced—in the daily life.

The disconnect between what we have learned and how well we function in these areas points us back to the need for spiritual discipleship and growth.

This path often forgets that Christians are formed through both the quality and quantity of time that eventually has space to address the real heart issues. We all desire time with people who can effectively speak to our souls, those who have the spiritual authority to speak life into our chaos. I should note that these heart issues can be brought to the surface and identified through programs, but the programs alone will never offer the depth of guidance, healing, and discipleship we all need.

Again, this path is not wrong in itself. The church should be practical and efficient in its offering of healthy programs. We need to think of ways to expose as many people to the faith as possible and figure out ways to disciple people in a harried culture. However, in doing so, we must not lose sight of the reality that discipleship in the end is not a pragmatic endeavor.

The greatest strength of the corporate model of discipleship is in the early phases; and, conversely, its greatest weakness becomes apparent in the longer, harder, and deeper stages. This path virtually ignores the inefficient and messy nature of discipleship and misses the need for a more individualized approach. It underestimates the time and intentionality needed to disciple another. In fact, it misses the incarnational nature of discipleship modeled by the master disciple maker, Jesus Christ.

If we measured Jesus' effectiveness in discipling others on the scales of our modern pragmatism He would be found wanting. We could actually criticize Jesus for not using His time wisely, for not being very efficient, and for not producing more disciples. In His three years of public ministry He could only hold onto twelve disciples, and one of them was a complete bust. Moreover, ten of the other eleven jumped ship when the waters got rough.

As silly as this critique seems, how much of this way of thinking exists collectively in the church? How much of our western mindset penetrates our thinking in unsuspected ways? Are we putting too much weight on short term metrics? I suggest as a remedy that we assume Jesus was the best person to disciple others and that His life and witness should be our guide as to how we disciple others. We know He commands us to go into the world and make disciples. Having seen His model, why do we ignore, abstain from, and otherwise reject some of the basic principles God Himself modeled?

While I will speak more fully about the incarnational nature of discipleship later, let me note here that the accounts in the Gospels plainly show that Jesus was intentional in choosing disciples and often rejected those who offered themselves as disciples. Jesus committed significant time to being with His disciples, as well as, to teaching and guiding them. He shared meals with them and walked with them. While He did teach the masses, He clearly poured Himself more completely into those He specifically chose as His disciples. He prayed for them; He counseled them; He shared His heart with them, and He loved them. In short, we see a very robust picture of Jesus' deep commitment to equip and train those disciples to make more disciples.

The Individualist Path

My experience in the church for the first eight years of my life as an adult Christian followed this pattern: I would hear a sermon or a teaching and then say to myself, "Okay, I understand the concept; now I will figure out how to live this out." Having understood the idea, my intention then was to figure out how to apply it in my life. I would start off with zeal, but all too often my efforts waned. When I ran into roadblocks and had no one to help me understand, I would abandon my efforts with a dose of shame in my failure.

"I can do it myself" and "just believe in yourself" are common themes in our culture. We encounter them in books, movies, stories, and other mediums. In the western world, even among Christians, individualism is celebrated as an admirable trait. We should not be surprised at how many of us end up on this individualistic path of discipleship.

In our faith journey and spiritual life, we often act as our own guide. We make decisions and order our lives based on what we think is best. We have blind spots. As we live in ignorance of these blind spots, we cause pain to ourselves and others. The idea of allowing a community of wise and caring believers with our best interests at heart to speak into our lives seems strange, perhaps even bordering on authoritarian to many. We must recognize that there is an unhealthy ignorance of how to connect with others and who could wisely disciple us. Unfortunately, a distrust of the system, the organization, the leaders in charge, and the church's ability to disciple us prevails.

Consequently, many of us decide to figure out how to live the Christian life on our own. We set our own agenda as to what we learn rather than following the agenda set by the broader community. Consumerism creeps in. We rationalize, "I will go where I am being fed. I will do what is best for my family and me, and I know what is best. No one is looking out for me, so I'd better do it myself." Again, the half-truths are always the ones that trip us up the most.

Ecclesiastes 4:9 tells us, "Two are better than one, because they have a good return for their labor." One of the things Jesus modeled clearly in dealing with His disciples was that He sent them out two by two. He always sent them out in groups. Even for a task as simple as finding a donkey, He sent two. There are many mysteries of the faith—this is just not one of them. Christianity is not a solo sport but a team game. The disciples understood this pattern and would always send at least two disciples on missionary journeys. Why do we think we can be disciples without the companionship and help of others?

We learn to be disciples in the context of community. People tend to react when I say, "Jesus was never alone." Nevertheless, the Bible confirms that whenever Jesus decided to get away from the crowd or His disciples, He was doing so to be with His Father. He was intentional about being with His Father in order to hear His Father's voice and fulfill His calling. His goal was never simply to have time to Himself. In short, He did not model discipleship as an individual pursuit. When we insist on doing it alone, we miss the fullness that comes from being in the Body of Christ, and we are not fully formed as disciples.

Another form of the individualist path that outwardly seems to care for others follows this pattern: I read a book, hear a sermon, or attend a retreat which draws me closer to God. Having encountered the Living God, I earnestly desire for others to have a similar experience. I subconsciously reason that what worked for me should work for others. This is not entirely faulty thinking for we should give testimony to the occasions where we encounter God. However, the problem comes when this is upheld as a must for discipleship.

This path fails to incorporate the uniqueness of the individual. What God wants me to learn today may not be what He wants those around me to learn. I should not extrapolate God's perfect timing for me to all others. God makes our experience holy by meeting us where we are and being present with us. The experience itself is not the holy thing. Pressuring or encouraging others to have the same experience simply is not life-giving.

The Unintentional Path

My friend Jimmy was what you would call a very laid-back guy. He had been a Christian for a decade, but his life never seemed to change much. He repeatedly struggled with the same issues and experienced minimal growth. When I finally had the guts to talk to him about his life, he explained, "I do not need to do anything to be a disciple because my labor will only become a form of works righteousness. God is provident and in charge of all my ways, and I will let the circumstances of my life unfold and trust the Lord is discipling me all the way."

Unfortunately, this lack of intentionality in discipleship is growing more and more prevalent. This path, as most, started with the good intentions of those who earnestly addressed the problem of thinking that anyone could work their way into the Kingdom. They were trying to shift the impetus of discipleship back to God.

This idea is right in that all good things emanate from God; however, this path goes too far in the other direction. Proponents of this path tend to eschew programs and systems. They are so distrustful of any talk of trying harder, making an effort, or running the good race that they dismiss all work as works righteousness.

What is left is a focus on God's responsibility in discipleship with a complete negation of our personal responsibility. In Matthew 19, a "rich young ruler" professed a desire to be a disciple of Jesus Christ; but, in the end, he was not willing to sacrifice his riches to follow Jesus. The offer was there from Jesus, but, at that point in His journey, he was unwilling to make the choice. Jesus did not fail him.

Proponents of this path unintentionally remove the necessity of intentionality in discipleship. They forget that discipleship has to do with putting on the full armor, running the race, fighting the good fight, and working out our salvation with fear and trembling. The true disciple says, "I want to learn, I want to grow, I want to have my heart changed and to be sanctified. I know I cannot do it in my own strength or through my own will, but I have heard that there is a savior who can show me a new way of living. I will find Him, I will seek Him, and I will do whatever it takes to get to Him. I will rip open a hole in the roof if He is within."

The Partial Path

One of my mentors inevitably would identify nearly every issue as a leadership problem. In the world he created, there were always opportunities to train as a leader, to take leadership development courses, and to help others develop as leaders.

Honestly, he usually seemed to be on the right track. He encouraged me to read leadership books and most of our conversations were about how to lead the church well. I remember asking him, "Is leadership really the core issue? I know leadership certainly is mentioned in the Bible, but a leadership development approach seems to leave out so many." He explained to me that he views every Christian as a leader on some level.

Later I realized that because the word "discipleship" has been misused and misunderstood in our culture, he had, like many in the church, developed a strategy for using more compelling terms to engage people in discipleship. Now, instead of saying "you need to be discipled," we say that you need some "coaching" or "leadership development" or "spiritual mentoring." The thought is that it is easier to get people engaged in these endeavors than to have them admit they need discipleship.

Although this renaming of discipleship comes out of a desire to do good, there are some unintended consequences to be considered. It is true that discipleship is so comprehensive that breaking it into understandable components is helpful. True discipleship certainly incorporates coaching, leadership, mentoring, spiritual formation, counseling, etc . . .

However, there are times when good questions are helpful and other times when we need those who have gone before us to mentor and teach us. There are times when we need to give or receive counsel from others in the body. The problem comes when we isolate the parts from the whole. We unintentionally and yet inevitably communicate that one component is more important or helpful than the others.

This contributes to the misunderstanding of discipleship as a whole. We end up with discipleship's being merely about leadership or prayer or mission or worship or fill in the blank. We end up with partial paths of discipleship, and that leaves us with disciples who feel incomplete and frustrated. We have deconstructed discipleship to better understand it but have not done the hard work of putting it back together again to make it complete.

This partial path is commonly centered on corporate worship. Certainly, Sunday morning gatherings are powerful and, used rightly, aid in discipleship. However, corporate worship cannot be a full substitute for discipleship. We cannot believe that exposing someone for a few hours a week to holy worship will be sufficient for his or her growth as a Christian.

The unintended consequence of breaking discipleship into components is that people tend to choose only the parts they like while leaving the rest unattended. This creates partially discipled Christians—and, this explains much of Christianity's decline in our culture.

The Superstar Path

I once was a convention and retreat junkie seeking out the latest and greatest author, church leader, or seminar. I thought that getting around the best and the brightest would help me be a better Christian. Only recently did I discard the piles of journals, workbooks, and CD's I had racked up over the years. You see, I finally realized that chasing after the superstar, the new and the novel did not actually translate into growth and maturity in my own life.

Naturally we are drawn to celebrities, heroes, and exemplars. Social media and the capitalist machine saturate our minds with promises of the next great book, teacher, leader, or program. We want to be discipled by the best, the brightest, the latest, and the most relevant. We want to grow.

We do not want to be discipled by some poor, old man who has never made a name for himself. We put the megachurch pastor on a pedestal. We hype the latest author. We attend the biggest or most elite conference. We think if we can get in with the superstar we will grow in our faith. We want to pick the most popular Christian to be our mentor. We look to the latest book, the largest church, and the biggest names to guide us. We spend enormous time and energy trying to get the best mentor, the best advice, the most well-known authority. Unfortunately, this path fuels an endless pursuit of the novel, leaving most Christians on this path exhausted.

In some ways following the famous Christian seems to make sense. After all, we reason, he or she must have learned something to have achieved such acclaim, but the superstar never has enough time to spend with you. The book can't answer the questions it leaves you with. The conference does not give you the space to figure out how to incorporate the teachings into your life in a healthy and balanced way.

In His day, Jesus committed to the twelve who were not the shining lights of society. He did not disciple the rich and famous. He built the firm foundation of the church with obscure men and women, and He changed the world. Discipleship starts locally, starts with who is willing, starts small, starts with each individual, and trusts that unheralded faithfulness bears the most fruit.

The Religious Path

I have to be honest with you—when someone says, "I am holding you accountable," it gives me pause. I have run into too many people interested in moral policing. We have too many people signing up to become Christian Pharisees. When discipleship gets reduced to a set of rules, we are in trouble.

Just as we see in Paul's letters to the Corinthians, even the early church was threatened by the Pharisaical spirit creeping into Christianity. Paul had to deal with Jews who wanted to make all the Gentiles receive circumcision. Paul reacted rather harshly against these men who were using an outward form of discipleship. He knew Christianity was not about following rules but about having a relationship with the ruler of all things.

The religious spirit remains because it taps into our desire to do something right. Many people today actually want to do discipleship right. They start out meaning well. They learn some form of discipleship, and they religiously take that form and apply it to all people in all circumstances. They believe if you follow this way, you will achieve success.

They reason that if you are not being discipled, it is because you are doing something wrong. We will always have to deal with the religious spirit. People will always turn discipleship into a methodology instead of something that is firmly rooted in relationship.

At the heart of the religious path of discipleship is the thought that there is a right way to do discipleship. If you follow these rules, you will get this result; if you do not, you are the problem. We wish that we could all follow a specific formula and achieve the desired results, but Jesus modeled a different way. He criticized the Pharisees for spreading that belief. We must be on the watch for falling into the same trap.

I have seen this path in many evangelical churches where right doctrine is equated with discipleship. If we can just believe the right things about God and explain how it all works, we have then become disciples. This over-rationalistic approach to discipleship leaves a wake of well-meaning Christians feeling judged and overwhelmed.

The religious path is also prevalent in traditional and liturgical church-es, even though the presentation may differ. I believe this comes from a noble pursuit to recapture what was lost in the Reformation. There has been a reawakening to liturgy, the church fathers, and the spiritual disciplines. Though this is a worthwhile pursuit, we need to guard against the tendency to worship the way we worship. We are tempted to think that following the right forms in the right way will lead to the development of the right kind of disciple. In His interactions with the religious leaders, Jesus cautioned that liturgy, rituals, and disciplines done without relationship lead to false and empty religious activity. (See Matthew 23.) Discipleship is much more than this.

IN CONCLUSION

Now, as we look at the way we approach the gardening of souls, we can identify some key barriers to good soil, namely: intellectualism, pragma-tism, individualism, narcissism, and institutionalism. These faulty and incomplete approaches to discipleship have been tried and found lacking.

In the following chapters, to help recapture the art of discipleship, let's examine the good soil that produces the desired fruit.

3

The Good Soil of Calling

ONGOING CYCLE OF DISCIPLESHIP

Calling
"Hearing God"

Community
"The Body of Christ"

Ministry
"The good works called to do"

Equipping
"Character and gifting"

STAY WITH ME NOW! Let's turn our attention to the solution and expand our vision of what is possible as mature disciples of Jesus Christ. In this chapter, let's examine the first and most essential ingredient in the good soil of discipleship—Calling.

Calling is where the Christian life starts. Listening to God and being obedient is at the heart of all discipleship. We were created to hear His voice, obey His commands, and be fathered by Him. We see this from the beginning in Genesis.

Before the Fall, God spoke with and instructed Adam and Eve on their work in creation. He taught them about the Garden and the animals. He would walk with them daily and disciple them as His children. Even after they had eaten from the tree of the knowledge of good and evil and had fallen into sin, "they heard the voice of the Lord God walking in the garden in the cool of the day" (Genesis 3:8a KJV). God still called to them, and they still heard His voice; however, they chose not to respond to His call. Instead, they tried to hide from Him, and all of mankind has been doing the same ever since. God continues to call to His children every day. Part of discipleship is learning the patterns and rhythms that allow us to hear from Him.

When the Son of Man took human form in the person of Jesus, He emphatically modeled for us the importance of heeding the call or voice of the Father continually. As we read in John 5:16–30, Jesus wanted us to understand that all of His actions proceeded from the instructions of the Father. He did not do things because they were good or right, but because the Father had called Him to do so. He understood that the Father would only instruct Him to do things that were good and right. We often get this backward and justify our labors because they are good and right. True disciples understand that we should only justify our action or inaction because the Father called us and led us in that way.

In Matthew 7:21–23, Jesus explained to Peter and the crowd the difference between true and false disciples. He told them that many would come to Him on the Day of Judgment and say, "Lord, Lord, did we not prophesy in your name and in your name drive out demons and in your name perform many miracles?" Then He stated that He would plainly say, "I never knew you. Away from me, you evildoers!" Jesus was driving home a critical point for His disciples. True discipleship is a response to God's call; true discipleship is doing what the Father tells us to do—no more and no less. Discipleship is not obeying rules or doing what is right in our own understanding. Too often we would rather not develop the discipline of hearing the voice of the Father but would choose instead to reduce our faith to religious practices. We get busy, hope that good works will suffice, and try justifying ourselves in a million ways. The net result is that we live outside of the call of God.

The good news is that God continues to pursue us—continues to call out to us. In fact, He came after us while we were still sinners (Romans 5:8). Just as God pursued Adam and Eve in Genesis 3 after they had disobeyed and hid from Him, He continues to pursue us. Now, because of what Jesus did for us on the cross, we can again hear, listen, and respond. This is the heart and start of discipleship.

Hearing from the perfect Father is not only the foundation of discipleship, it is also the wellspring of joy. Outward circumstances can produce pleasure and sometimes happiness, but true joy comes from hearing the Father and, in spite of any circumstances, knowing you are loved and secure in His heart.

I will never forget Gene because he lived a life worth living. He had confidence that he was doing what he was created to do. He lived a courageous life that seemed both satisfying and fruitful. He did not have a charismatic personality, he was not glamorous, and he never craved attention. Gene seemed to know when to act and when to wait. He had a peace that circumstances did not seem to shake. He lived a life worth emulating.

Gene was a husband, father, and physician, but, more importantly, he was a son of the Most High. He died way too soon, but his life inspired me to live a life worth living. People who live in accord with their callings should be our Christian heroes. This kind of life is what we yearn for. If we would actually believe that this kind of life was possible, we would be willing to sacrifice much to possess that kind of clarity. Frankly, we see this calling on one's life lived out in its purest form in the life and death of Jesus Christ.

Calling is about the story of our individual lives. Calling is where we hear from God and begin to see how our story is grafted into His story. (See Romans 11:17.) We drastically underestimate the power of the stories we tell ourselves. Our internal story influences our behavior, emotional state, and decision-making. The Christian life is learning the real story, the true story of God and who we are and how He continues to call us into the great story.

Our initial sense of calling is often when we first understand what Jesus did for us through His life, death, and resurrection. We accept this reality and receive Him as our Lord and Savior. This is our conversion story. This is where His story intersects and converges with our story.

While conversion is vitally important, we must understand that this is only the start of His call on our lives, not the end. When we become Christians, we receive access to our heavenly Father. When Jesus rose from the dead, the curtain in the temple was torn in two from top to bottom. That which separated us from His presence was removed giving us uninterrupted access to our Creator. It is important to understand that His calling continues throughout our entire Christian life. This understanding of continuous calling undergirds true discipleship. At the heart of discipleship is the ongoing hearing of God's voice followed by the choice to follow. He will never stop coming to us to reveal His will for our lives.

To fully understand calling you need to understand that there are varying timeframes and depths of calling. There is the daily calling of hearing God's voice in prayer or in reading of scripture that puts you in His path each day. There is seasonal calling in terms of your work and ministry. I was called to be a teacher, then youth minister, then a church planter, and then a leadership coach. There are ongoing callings like being a husband or a mother that last decades and often for life.

There are callings for a specific task like speaking a word of encouragement to someone in distress; and, there are deeper callings like knowing the Father more intimately and trusting Him with all your fears and concerns. What is common is that they all have at their source God, and God wants you to hear His voice and know His will for your life.

Let's look at the call of some of the biblical disciples to see the ongoing nature of God's calling.

THE CALL OF PETER

Peter was a rough and tough fisherman in the region of Galilee. He was a man who took responsibility for his life. He worked hard and had some set rhythms of life. That is until Jesus called.

> As Jesus was walking beside the Sea of Galilee, He saw two brothers; Simon called Peter and his brother Andrew. They were casting a net into the lake, for they were fishermen. "Come, follow me," Jesus said, "and I will send you out to fish for people." At once they left their nets and followed him. (Matthew 4:18–20)

Wow! Jesus encountered Peter and said, "Hey, stop doing what you have always been doing and follow me. You have been called to be a fisherman but do not settle for catching fish only. If you follow me, you will change the lives of men and women" (author's version).

Peter heard the voice of Jesus and responded in obedience. This was the first call on his life to become a Christ-follower. He never forgot that day, that moment when everything changed. We do not get a lot of details, but we do know that this was just the beginning of his calling.

As we look at the next three years of his discipleship, Peter was continuing to learn to respond to the calling of God, to hear and obey the voice of Jesus. In Matthew 10:1, we read, "Jesus called his twelve disciples to him and gave them authority to drive out impure spirits and to heal every disease and sickness." Jesus repeatedly called Peter unto Himself. Jesus was teaching Peter to hear His voice, know what to do, and have the power and authority to accomplish what God asked of him. We can be certain Peter's calling included many questions, long discussions, and instruction.

> As Peter grew as a disciple, we can see his increased understanding of the power of the call of Jesus. When Peter saw Jesus walking on water, Peter's response was remarkable: And when the disciples saw him walking on the sea, they were troubled, saying, It is a spirit; and they cried out for fear. But straightway Jesus spake unto them, saying, Be of good cheer; it is I; be not afraid. And Peter answered him and said, Lord, if it be thou, bid me come unto thee on the water. And he said, Come. And when Peter was come down out of the ship, he walked on the water, to go to Jesus. (Matthew 14:26–29 KJV)

Peter saw Jesus walking on the water through a storm and responded that if Jesus called him, he would step out of the boat and walk on the water as well. We remember what happened—Peter took his attention off Jesus, looked at the waves on the sea, and started to sink. Too often, this is the part of the story we focus on—namely, that when we take our gaze off Jesus, we sink. That is surely true; and, we all take our eyes off Jesus on a regular basis allowing circumstances to batter us. However, the amazing part of this story to me is that Peter was willing to get out of the boat.

In that incident, Peter knew something about calling. He learned that the only way to do the impossible was if Jesus called you to do it. He saw that there was a deep power in the call of God that changes circumstances. Peter boldly modeled the heart of discipleship. He recognized where the power resided. He did not just jump out of the boat and say, "Well, if You can do it, I can too." No, he said, "If and only if You call me, will I step out of my fear and trust You that I can do the impossible . . . that I can walk on water."

This primacy of call is what opens the door to discipleship. We all face trials and experience pain. We are all tempted to focus on them instead of the call of Jesus. But if we are willing to do what Jesus calls us to do, we will overcome fear. The result is that the impossible becomes possible. Jesus tells us that we will do greater things than He if we follow His calling for our lives. (See John 14:12.)

Calling is about being in such an intimate relationship with the Lord that we are willing to listen to His voice, trust Him, and rely on Him to equip us. This pattern requires the practice of abiding in the Lord and returning to Him when we wander and rebel. Peter had to learn this truth. In Matthew 17, Jesus called Peter to accompany Him up the mountain where He subsequently was transfigured. In response to seeing Jesus transfigured, Peter came up with a plan. Notice that he did run this plan by Jesus before he acted.

> "Lord, it is good for us to be here. If you wish, I will put up three shelters—one for you, one for Moses and one for Elijah." While he [Peter] was still speaking, a bright cloud covered them, and a voice from the cloud said, "This is my Son, whom I love; with him I am well pleased. Listen to him!" (Matthew 17:4–5)

Like us, Peter was not perfect. He still had his own ideas of how things should work, but more importantly, he was learning to "check in" with Jesus before acting. Peter wisely prefaced his plan with "if you wish." He was a disciple and was learning to make sure his ideas and actions lined up with that of the calling of Jesus. Peter knew that the calling of God was ongoing and that as a disciple of Christ, he must attend to it on a regular basis.

God knows we all have a tendency to do life our way. God knows we would rather do what we want without conferring with Him. Notice Peter did not actually build three shelters. He had grown as a disciple and, in this case, did not act before making sure it was the will of God. Peter was aware of a past pattern of behavior of acting on his own ideas. Now in this instance, he was being made new and tried to capture his thoughts to discern if the idea was actually from the Lord.

In this scene, God the Father underscores this point by saying that Jesus is His son and that we need to listen to Him. Like Peter, we may have a hard time believing that Jesus is actually speaking to us regularly and that He is calling to us daily.

Peter seemed to have understood the heart of discipleship. In reality, as Jesus approached His death, Peter became a bit overconfident. He boldly denied that he would ever leave Jesus, and Jesus responded that Peter would deny Him three times that very day. Wow! The disciple whom Jesus spent the most time with abandon Him? How could that be? What did this mean? The meaning was and is that in our humanity we will struggle to hear the voice of God and obey.

Like us, Peter was dismayed. He thought he had failed as a disciple. After Jesus died, Peter returned to his old life as a fisherman, but Jesus appeared to Peter and called him back. In John 21, Jesus called to him from shore. Peter's reaction was priceless. Upon hearing the voice of Jesus, Peter recognized Him, jumped from the boat, and swam to Jesus on the shore. All the training of listening to the call of Jesus had worked. Even after His death on the cross, Peter was aware of the voice of Jesus when he heard it. Just as quickly as he had gone back to his old life, he responded to the voice of Jesus calling.

Disciples develop that keen ability to know the voice of the Lord even in unexpected times and places. As disciples, we often return to old ways of living, but we learn to jump ship and return to Him when we hear His voice. Calling is ongoing. Responding to the call is what disciples do.

As Peter continued to mature as a disciple, Jesus called to him in a dream. At first, Peter pushed back because he did not fully understand. What the Lord was calling him to do seemed strange. God was calling him to take the gospel to the Gentiles. For a Jew, this was unthinkable! In that culture, Gentiles were unclean and should be avoided. Peter knew that if he treated Gentiles as equals, there would be serious repercussions. He knew that responding to the call of God was dangerous, but He listened to the voice of God and obeyed. He was living as a disciple.

THE CALL OF PAUL

Before he was the disciple Paul, he was Saul. Saul was one of the elites. He was highly educated and respectable. He was a man with power and authority. When he spoke, people listened and followed. He was a full Roman citizen with all of its rights and privileges. He was an up and coming superstar in the Jewish faith, a religious leader who was going somewhere. As a man of action, he was looking to make a name for himself, and he did this by actively persecuting Christians.

Soon after the death and resurrection of Jesus, the Jews identified those who heeded the call of Jesus as a dangerous cult that must be stopped. Saul volunteered to lead a movement to kill Christians, but even the murderer Saul was not beyond the call of God.

Saul was on his way to Damascus to kill more Christians when he was struck down and blinded by God. In this dramatic story, God called out and asked Saul, "Why are you persecuting me?" (Acts 9:4 ESV).

Though blinded, Saul (who is called Paul) could actually see, for the first time, that Jesus was the Savior of the world—the one whom all Jews had been awaiting. Paul was humbled and fell to the ground, forever changed. He heard the call of God and chose to listen. Afterward, he realized that God had always been calling him: "But when he who had set me apart before I was born, and who called me by his grace, was pleased to reveal his Son to me . . ." (Galatians 1:15 ESV).

Paul had a dramatic conversion and started preaching. In fact, he preached in Damascus in the synagogues until they tried to kill him. He then went to Jerusalem and preached there, but his reputation had preceded him. Christians were not sure they could trust this man who had recently been leading the pack of men trying to kill them. Realizing that Paul needed to be discipled, the leaders of the church sent him back to his hometown in Tarsus, where he would spend years being an unknown disciple before going on his famous missionary journeys.

Paul was like so many of us when we respond to the initial call of God—gung-ho! He was ready to charge, to take the hill, to go public immediately. Good thing God loved him too much to let him loose! Instead, Paul spent years in obscurity learning the basics of being a disciple. He learned the lessons in his everyday life that eventually would make him so effective in his writing that his letters to various churches would become scripture.

Paul responded to his initial call, but that was not the final word. God kept calling him. In Acts, we find out that Barnabas went to Tarsus and called Paul to minister with him and teach the new Christians in Antioch. So, Paul became a disciple who would disciple others. Paul spent a year in Antioch teaching and giving away all that he had been learning as a disciple in the previous decade in his hometown.

God never stopped calling to Paul. Later, he was "called to be an apostle of Christ Jesus by the will of God" (1 Corinthians 1a). This apostolic call was instructing Paul to do the work of going out to new cities, starting new churches, and preaching the gospel to the Gentiles. Paul had been trained and equipped and now was being released into a new season of calling, a calling to be a missionary.

Paul was faithful to this call and went on a series of missionary journeys. Listen to what happened as he tried to live out this call:

> And they went through the region of Phrygia and Galatia, having been forbidden by the Holy Spirit to speak the word in Asia. And when they had come up to Mysia, they attempted to go into Bithynia, but the Spirit of Jesus did not allow them. So, passing by Mysia, they went down to Troas. And a vision appeared to Paul in the night: a man of Macedonia was standing there, urging him and saying, "Come over to Macedonia and help us." And when Paul had seen the vision, immediately we sought to go on into Macedonia, concluding that God had called us to preach the gospel to them. (Acts 16:6–10 ESV)

Paul, like all of us, had made plans which he thought made some sense. He thought going to the province of Asia to spread the gospel seemed like a good idea, but God had a different plan. Paul was prevented by the Spirit of Jesus from going to Asia. Paul had to discern the call on his life for that season and concluded that he was actually called to go to Macedonia instead.

This was the ongoing discipleship of Paul. He still had to tune into the voice of God for direction and instruction. He still had his own ideas and had to learn to discern if they were in alignment with God's. Even for a seasoned disciple like Paul, his plans were not always in alignment with his calling. Knowing he was called of God was an important aspect of discipleship to strengthen Paul through much persecution in the form of beatings, death threats, and prison. Such opposition could have led him to abandon his course of action had he not been clear about God's leading. Most of our plans usually do not include such painful experiences, yet we are tempted to walk away from what we have been called to do.

When Paul was in Corinth, he was afraid for his life and wondered if he should leave the city. God called to Paul and Paul obeyed.

> "Do not be afraid; keep on speaking, do not be silent. For I am with you, and no one is going to attack and harm you, because I have many people in this city." So, Paul stayed in Corinth for a year and a half, teaching them the word of God. (Acts 18:9b–11)

Paul never had all the answers, but he was willing to listen to the one who did. We must never get out of the habit of listening to the voice and call of God. Living out our calling is the only way of living as a Christian that brings us abundant life. God is speaking, and as His children, we must undertake and develop the habit of listening and obeying.

MY CALLING

I am certainly no Peter or Paul, but let me share with you how I have wrestled with calling in my life. I was born in a family that went to church most Sundays until my parents got divorced. Then we stopped. As a middle school student, the message I picked up was that when things were going bad, the church was not the place for you. I thought I should get my life together before going back to church.

However, God was calling me. When I was a punk teenager doing whatever I wanted. God, used two of my closest friends to invite me to a weekend retreat where the gospel was being presented. At this retreat, we were exposed to the gospel in multiple ways, not only in verbal presentation but also in action. The community was loving us, praying for us, and overwhelming us with generosity. I was wooed by the incredible love of the Living God and made a commitment to become a Christian.

Through high school and into college I had a foot in two worlds. I would go to Bible studies with my girlfriend and also party on the weekends. In terms of the world, I was doing well. I was accepted to medical school at age nineteen, was in the Honors college at USC, and was a national officer for my fraternity. When asked to be on a panel for success, I accepted the opportunity with pride and spoke with groups on what it took to be successful.

In my sophomore year of college in the midst of much worldly success, I was miserable. I was in charge of my life. I was making the calls. However, though it looked good on the outside, on the inside I knew I was out of control. At that point, my girlfriend broke up with me, obviously not deceived by the hype about how successful I was. In my misery, it occurred to me that if this was all the world had to offer, it sure was lame! Maybe the abundant life God was offering might be the way to go.

It was then that God clearly called me to come under His Lordship. I knew He was my Savior, but I had not been willing to let Him be Lord in directing my ways. I wanted to hold the reins, but the truth finally registered with me. He was calling me to trust Him with my life, with my decisions, with everything I had. It was a dramatic moment, which started a shift in the way I ordered my life. In the call to follow Him as Lord, God had invited me to walk with Him, talk to Him, and to listen to Him.

Nevertheless, it was not an overnight change. At nineteen, I had applied and been accepted into medical school. Since it had seemed like a good idea to be a doctor, I continued with that plan. It was a key life decision about my future that I had made without knowing God's call on my life.

At twenty-one and in medical school, I was praying regularly for strength. I knew something was not right. Then in September of 1989, Hurricane Hugo hit Charleston, and the Medical University of South Carolina was temporarily shut down.

In the week following the hurricane, in the midst of chopping down trees, cooking food on the grill with all the neighbors, and helping others cope with their losses, the Holy Spirit finally got through to me. I recognized that God did not want me to pursue medicine. Through prayer, conversation with Christian friends, and an honest assessment of my gifting I "heard" God calling me to a life as an ordained pastor.

The fact that I was not called to a vocation in medicine should have been obvious to me. It was to those around me. I do not like hospitals. I have little interest in biology. Watching videos of operations in medical school made me feel sick. I often faint at the sight of blood, and I am not good at details. I only liked the idea of being a physician. I did not actually like the idea of living the life of a physician.

My decision to go to medical school did not proceed from a calling but rather a decision that I made in isolation that seemed good to me at the time. God used a hurricane to give me space to listen again to His call. As a result, I was off to seminary.

My denomination sent me to a liberal seminary. I had professors who did not believe in the resurrection of Jesus Christ much less any miracles that He performed while on earth. Some professors mocked me as "Bible Boy" because I was constantly challenging their views with scripture. As I prayed about why God had allowed me to be sent to this place, it became clear that God was training me to stand in my faith in the midst of intellectual and spiritual attacks on the faith that had been entrusted to the early church.

While in seminary preparing for a life in ministry, I struggled with God about having a wife. I had dated three great Christian women, and for some reason, I never sensed a call to marry any of them. My friends accused me of fear of commitment. While there may have been some truth to that, I also knew God had not opened the door.

At twenty-seven, being often lonely, I wanted to marry and have a family, but nothing seemed to be happening on that front. Clearly, I was asking God to bless my will for my life instead of seeking His will for my life. Eventually, I was able to lay my desires at the foot of the cross and surrendering said, "Lord, your will not mine." Within a week of this surrender, I met Louise. From the beginning, we hit it off. We took long walks on the beach where we talked naturally about the things that mattered to us—and they were the same things. We spent as much time together as possible simply because we enjoyed each other's company so much. Within four months, it was clear to me that God was calling me to marriage. It took Louise a little longer to get to this point, but that is another story. Eventually we married.

After two years of marriage, Louise became pregnant. Obviously, the Lord was calling me to fatherhood and quickly! We had three sons in three years while I was planting a church. On the one hand, what a gift and answer to prayer! On the other hand, this calling required me to confront how selfish I really was. The amount of sacrifice and servanthood required with three infants who constantly needed to have their diapers changed, to be fed, put to bed, clothed, etc., came as a shock! The calling to Fatherhood was a calling to grow in character—to be honest about who I was and was not. It was learning to put the needs and care of others above my own with no thanks forthcoming. In fact, it would take a whole book to tell of the life lessons God has taught me through my children.

In my mid-thirties, I had just finished a doctorate in ministry and was ready to do great things for God. However, I soon found myself in a dark period. My brother was tragically murdered, I had no job offers, and I was a wreck. I could not believe I had been as successful as I was, and no one wanted to hire me.

So, Louise and I packed up our three young children and moved to Charleston, South Carolina, to be close to family. To pay the bills, I accepted a job raising money for a good cause; but I was not using my gifts, nor did it feel like I was living out my calling. This was depressing! It took all the energy I could muster simply to get up each morning and go to work. I remember asking the Lord every day on my commute why He would prepare me to be a pastor and not provide a job.

As I prayed daily in great frustration, pressing into God over and over in that wilderness season, I finally heard His call. His response was clear. He was calling me into greater intimacy with Him. I would find out that this intimacy would require some healing of my soul.

In that season, He called me to deal with the judgment that was in my heart. The Lord knew I had to deal with my long-term internal issues before He could use me in the next season of ministry. This was a season of repentance and healing. In His mercy, God gave me time to deal with this before I moved into my next assignment.

God took me out of ministry through circumstances and showed me how much judgment was hurting me and those around me, and how to receive healing. He discipled me so that I was ready to respond to my next vocation. I would need to be able to love and serve Christian leaders without having judgment towards them. In short, this call was a call to deeper intimacy with Him. By the end of that year, God opened doors for me to go back into full-time pastoral ministry.

Once again in ministry, I was planting a church, working on teaching pastors, and honing my leadership skills. I knew more than ever that I was called to step into that which God had prepared in advance for me to do. (See Ephesians 2:10.) As I worked, I was gaining more clarity on my call, but my fears were increasing. Although I was happy to be back working as a pastor, I was working three jobs to make ends meet. I knew I needed to pare down my responsibilities. I was working hard to please three bosses instead of doing what the Father told me.

Although I was excited about my calling and the clarity of stewarding my gifts, I had a gnawing concern that if I communicated to my bosses what God had called me to do, I might be rejected. I might lose a job. Those whom I worked for might have replied, "That sounds great. I am glad you are clear on what you should do. The only problem is that we are not paying for that."

At that point, I needed to decide whether I was going to please men so that I could get provide for my family or whether I was going to trust God to provide for our needs. I knew the world might not value my call; however, with much encouragement, I made the commitment to speak to all my bosses about the direction I thought the Lord was leading me. I was overwhelmed with joy when God opened the doors for me. The three jobs became one full-time job.

In my forties, I wrestled with how to father my three teenage boys. My father was not around for my teenage years, so I had no model. I was not sure what a godly fathering of teenagers looked like. Was I being too lax or too strict? I waffled between too much discipline or too much grace. As I prayed about this, I felt compelled to press deeper into what it meant for me to live as an adopted son of the Father. Understanding how to be a son of my heavenly Father would equip me to better father my sons.

Up to that point, I had related to God as Lord and Savior but not much as Father. God was calling me to step into the fullness of Sonship. I reread scripture with a focus on Sonship, and again God discipled me in this new calling. I was being called to be a son and let God be my Father which in turn gave me insight on how to father well.

At age forty-three, I was out with some friends. Andy, who was not able to have children, was telling us that he had adopted a child just a week before and then just the day before our conversation had found out that his wife was pregnant. Andy went on to say how blessed he was and hoped for many more children. Some of my friends said, "Wait until you have three. You'll change your mind!" But, for some reason I responded, "Andy, I have never met anyone on their death bed who wished they had fewer children. Have as many as you can!" Twenty minutes later I was home, and my wife was telling me she was pregnant. We were starting afresh. Thankfully God had prepared me with the prior conversation by giving me the perspective to balance out the shock. God's calling on me as Father was going to last a lot longer than I had planned.

Now in my fifties, I am living out my calling to coach leaders. It is very satisfying to have the opportunity to use my gifts, but I wish that this ministry would grow. My limitations, both internal and external, frustrate me. As I took this frustration to God, He revealed that He is calling me to a season to be like Joseph in jail—not to promote myself or try to control my circumstances. God is calling me to live under the easy yoke of Christ. I am starting to understand how much I am under the illusion that I can do things in my own strength. I am learning how many things I did unyoked with Christ and how hard they were on me as I carried the whole weight of the burden. His call is one of greater dependence on Him, a call to live a life fully surrendered to His will. In fact, the writing of this book is an act of obedience. I do not like to write, and I do not think I am particularly gifted in the art. But I sensed a call to write down what I have learned about discipleship as an act of stewardship. God blessed me to be a blessing so that everything He has given me I want to give away.

I now expect His call on my life to continue; I understand that the call sometimes involves doing and other times involves learning to be with Him more fully. I have more expectation that He is speaking and that He will give me ears to hear. Calling never stops; it takes on many forms, sometimes in huge life-changing moments and other times in simple daily obedience. Being in relationship with God is about hearing His voice; and, hearing His voice is the calling on our lives.

Calling from God ultimately motivates, encourages, and challenges us to live fully connected to Him. Where do we practice listening to what God is calling us to do? What do we do when the circumstances of life overwhelm us? Do we retreat in fear or walk on the water when Jesus bids us? Are we living a life devoid of calling becoming more desperate, lonely, and ultimately so depressed that we are overwhelmed by a sense of angst?

Clarity of calling is an ongoing issue for Christians. We are constantly asking and contending with the "why" question of life. This drives our actions and thoughts. Discerning our calling starts with two questions: Where have I been and what has God been doing? The basis of calling is that God prepares us in advance for the things He has called us to do. (See Ephesians 2:10.) What is God preparing you for? What is your story? How has He shaped you through people, events and circumstances? What are your key values and life lessons? What are key Biblical verses or heroes that guide your life?

How do you continue to hear from God when He calls you? Through others? Through His word? Through circumstances? We see God using all of these methods to call disciples. Learning to discern God's voice in this way is a lifelong journey. We need help, we need encouragement, we need guidance, and we need to be discipled in responding to God's call.

In the next chapter, let's dig in the soil that gives greater definition to our calling. We will explore some key habits and rhythms that bring God's purposes into greater clarity. We will also look at the habits that keep us away from that calling

4

Working the Soil of Calling

CALLING IS ABOUT STORY. Story is how we are grafted into God's people, and your story is powerful. Tilling and working the soil is the part of discipleship that involves gaining clarity on your story and understanding how your story dovetails with God's story.

One of my favorite movie clips comes from the movie, *Mr. Holland's Opus*.[1] In this particular scene, Mr. Holland is reflecting on his life. Twenty-five years prior, he had begun teaching music at a high school as a means to pay the bills while following his dream to compose. Now he loves teaching music and he loves his students. Unfortunately, the school is eliminating the music program in an effort to reduce the budget. He believes he is being forced into early retirement. As he sits in his classroom for the last time, a friend walks in to find him brooding. The following conversation ensues:

BILL (*friend and football coach*): Hey.

MR. HOLLAND: Hey, what are you doing here?

Bill: I just came by to see if you need any help (*packing*).

MR. HOLLAND: (*despairingly*) No . . . no . . .

BILL: Do you know what you are going to do?

MR. HOLLAND: I am too old to start a rock band. Probably hang out a shingle and teach a few piano lessons.

1. *Mr. Holland's Opus*, by Patrick Sheane Duncan, directed by Stephen Herek, Hollywood Pictures, 1995.

BILL: I would love to retire.

MR. HOLLAND: I'm not retiring, Bill. I'm getting dumped and I don't think you have anything to worry about. The day they cut the football budget in this state, well now, that will be the end of Western civilization as we know it. Tell you the truth I'm scared to death.

BILL: They have no idea how much they will miss you around here.

MR. HOLLAND: You really think so?

BILL: What do you doubt it?

MR. HOLLAND: As a matter of fact, I do. Funny thing. I got dragged into this kicking and screaming and now it's the only thing I want to do. You work your whole life; you work for thirty years because you think that what you do makes a difference . . . think it matters to people. Then you wake up one morning and you find out well you know you made a little error, that you are expendable . . . Oh, God . . .

Mr. Holland was scared to death because he did not know his calling. And, because he did not know his calling, he felt subject to circumstances. He saw himself as a victim and considered himself unimportant and expendable. He believed others could keep him from doing what he was created to do.

Though this is a fictional character, I surmise that his real calling was to help others enjoy and play music so that its power and beauty could be experienced by many.

Sure, he did this as a music teacher, but he could have fulfilled his calling in many other ways. Sadly, he did not know that God's calling is never subject to the whims and fancies of circumstances or culture. Jesus fully lived into His calling even though He was persecuted, mocked, abused, and rejected by many.

As disciples of Christ, we must understand that it is a continuous struggle to seek His voice, to heed His calling and to have the courage to be faithful to our calling. Scripture sums this up by instructing us to "make every effort to confirm your calling and election. For if you do these things, you will never stumble" (2 Peter 1:10b).

HABIT AND RHYTHMS OF CALLING

Let's look at some key ideas, rhythms, and habits that foster clarity in understanding God's call. This is digging in the garden. This is cultivating the soil. This is our part in the equation. We are responsible for cultivation and God gives the growth.

Intentionality

Over time I have developed an important habit. This habit grew out of a series of failures. My common failing was allowing the bulk of my thoughts and actions to come as a response to someone, something, or some circumstance that had not yet happened.

I was overworking, over-thinking, and stressed. My schedule was completely reactionary. Complaining more and increasingly dissatisfied with my work, I was entering stage one burnout and knew I needed help.

Thankfully, my friend Terry helped me. He coached me to intentionally bring my time, energy, and focus into sync with my calling. I had to stop, reflect, and then order my day and my calendar around the things I was called to do. This required effort and planning. However, as I became proactive and intentional in stewarding all that I am in accordance with my calling, I began to experience abundant life.

Modern life has become so full of activity with so many options and incredibly diverse opportunities supplied via technology that most feel that adding something to their already full schedule is at best a burden and for many impossible. So, when we as Christians hear about taking discipleship seriously, our immediate thought is, "Where on earth am I going to be able to fit more into my already packed schedule?"

First, we must realize that much training in discipleship can be done in our current activities. Discipleship is not doing different things but doing the things we do differently. Secondly, yes, you will need to prioritize your time and make sacrifices to become a disciple of Christ.

Being intentional about your calling will take effort. You will have to be intentional about listening to the Lord. You will have to work with others to help clarify and refine your calling. You must choose to be accountable to your commitment to live into and courageously stick with your calling. Furthermore, calling does not become clear if you're walking alone. You need others to help in the process and that takes intentionality in finding out who is equipped to help you.

As Christians, we need to be intentional in creating time to hear from the Lord. We need to develop daily rhythms like quiet times, monthly rhythms of reflection, and yearly rhythms of protracted retreats aimed at gaining clarity from the Lord with the help of others. If you do not have a plan and are not intentional, more often than not, you lose will any sense of calling.

How are you intentional in getting clarity of calling? When do you set aside time for this? Who is helping you? What rhythms do you have to revisit your understanding of your calling? Who has affirmed your calling within the body?

Understanding Personal Responsibility

Personal responsibility originated in the Garden before the Fall. God placed Adam and Eve in the Garden and took ultimate responsibility for providing everything they needed. He gave them food for substance, one another for community, and finally His presence as He walked with them in the cool of the day. However, God relinquished to them the personal responsibility of tending the Garden. Adam and Eve had to gather, prepare and place the food in their mouths to get the nourishment they needed. They needed to show up and seek God as they walked in the Garden. Similarly, God expects you to participate in the ongoing process of discerning and following your calling.

After the Fall, work and provision became harder, relationships with one another became strained, and intimacy with God was broken. Again, God took ultimate responsibility. He sent His Son that we might be forgiven and our relationship with God restored. We can now live with one another in peace, joy, and love. God continues to provide all we need.

Still, we do have personal responsibility. We have a responsibility to respond to Christ's death on the cross and His invitation to turn to Him as Savior and Lord. We have a responsibility to be in community with our brothers and sisters in Christ, and we have a responsibility to do the work He has prepared in advance for us to do.

There are two equal and opposite errors made with this principle of personal responsibility. One fallacy is that we have no responsibility in following our calling because everything is beyond our control. We simply go through life and address what comes our way. We reason that if God wants us to live into our calling, it is His responsibility; therefore, there is little we can do to change our circumstances. We then grow idle in our pursuit of calling and get swept up in the current of the broken world; thus, we become fully disconnected from the call on our lives.

In our culture, the lie of diminishing personal responsibility looms large. It is easy to believe our condition is someone else's fault and out of our control which leaves many of us feeling like victims. The problem with this lie, like all effective lies, is that it is partially true. Others' actions do affect us; others intentionally or unintentionally do us harm. People deceive, friends betray, and spouses hurt one another; but the truth is that none of this can separate us from the life God has called us to live.

Conversely, when we realize personal renewal precedes the changes in our circumstances, we seek God for clarity instead of focusing on changing our circumstances, our job, our church, or our spouse.

The second error we make reasons that God has done all He is going to do; therefore, we are now fully responsible for following our calling. We take on God's ultimate responsibility for our welfare. We believe we have to take care of ourselves or no one else will. We take on full responsibility for clarifying the details of our calling and shoulder the burden of this task. We do not partner with God. We just work more and try harder. We are not yoked with Christ. We take on the full burden of life and head out on path that leads to burnout.

What is your personal responsibility within your relationship with God? What are you responsible for in your daily life? What is God responsible for in your life? Are you letting Him do that, or do you find yourself taking on His role? How do God's call and your personal responsibility dovetail in your experience?

Reflecting on Your Past

I remember the first time I did a timeline exercise. The assignment was to write out the 60–70 most important events, people, and circumstances of my life on colored sticky notes and put them in chronological order. At first, this seemed like it would be a waste of time. I already knew my past, my story. Why did I need to revisit it over and over? The value didn't become apparent until afterward when I realized that few exercises have helped me more to remember that God has always been at work in my life;

that He uses even the things the enemy desired for evil for good; and, that remembering what the Lord has done strengthens me to do the things He is calling me to do. Jeremiah 29:11 reads, "'For I know the plans I have for you,' declares the LORD, 'plans to prosper you and not to harm you, plans to give you hope and a future.'"

The last part of the verse reiterates the intention of God's plans. God has two goals in mind. The first is "a future." The Hebrew word is aharit. H. W. Wolff explains that it literally means "afterward, backwards or after part." So, how can it be about the future? The Hebrew concept of time is like a man rowing a boat. He sees where he has been, but the future is toward his back. As he focuses on set points in the past, he backs into the future. The future is entirely unknown to him because it is behind him!".[2]

This presents a powerful theological idea. First, God must set our course since only He can see ahead of us. But secondly, we have as our guide what we see, the course we have been following. We see the past because we are facing the past. The past is "before" us. No wonder our history with God is so important. Our story is not just about where we came from. Our story is the visible guide for our course into the future. Finally, there is a great connection with the idea that we must trust God's direction and not fear. If we are "backing" into the future, we must trust the guide. We cannot see where we are going, but He can.

So much of our life seems consumed with plans for our future. We all want to "look ahead" as though we will be able to guide and protect ourselves from what may come, but God says that the real direction of our life comes from the past. The course of our life was set in the past. The victory over the future happened in the past. It is our history with God that gives us peace and confidence.

Scripture often reminds us to stop and remember—remember what God has done, remember God's promises, and remember where you have been before you decide on where you think He is leading you. Remember God uses people, places, events, and circumstances to serve as guideposts as He leads us into the future.

The story of your life is powerful—it gives meaning and is an account of God's preparation for your future. When do you stop and remember? When do you reflect on your life? Can you see God at work even during the dark times of your life? How has God used the circumstances of your life to prepare you to live into your calling?

2. https://www.skipmoen.com/2009/06/a-look-at-jeremiah-2911/

Knowing Your Calling Emanates from Relationship

My son is pursuing a philosophy major in college. He is being taught two unhelpful world views. The first one is a materialism which purports that science provides all that we can know.

The second is worse. He is being taught you cannot really know anything for sure. Truth is purely subjective. Every thought we have is subject to personal biases and cannot be trusted.

Thankfully, in his heart, he understands that these worldviews taken at their core would lead anyone to despair and hopelessness.

We all understand what it means to know someone. Knowing my wife is not a careful study of her weight, height, hair color, and other physical attributes. Rather, knowing her is intimately understanding her story, sharing experiences, discussing her thoughts, ideas, feelings, and dreams. To love my wife and to know her drives me closer in our relationship.

Similarly, Christianity teaches that knowing emanates from relationship. While we can know truth and know who God is from scripture, we can know God intimately through relationship. God's call on our lives is discerned by being in relationship with Him. The good news of the gospel is that even though we are still sinful and broken vessels God desires to be with us, walk with us, and talk with us. He wants a relationship and delights in being with us.

As we look at Jesus' life, we see that He walked with those who broke the rules. He gave hope to those who were considered unclean and unworthy by the religious leaders; and, He renewed the idea that God constantly seeks and calls us.

If He wants to be with the tax collector, the prostitute, the loose women, the murderers, and the thieves, might He also want to be with you? When do you take time to be with the Father to get clarity on what to do? Do you do only what the Father tells you to do, or do you fill your life with work you are not called to do? Do you believe He delights in spending time with you? Do you delight in time spent with Him?

Learning to Hear from God

We constantly contend with the voices of our flesh, the world, and the devil. Kallistos Ware in his book, *The Orthodox Way*, notes that the heart of prayer is the ability to listen to God. He quotes an ancient text, "The Sayings of the Desert Fathers," to explain just how hard a task this is:

> Then brethren asked Abba Agathon: "Amongst all our different activities, father, which is the virtue that requires the greatest effort?" He answered, "Forgive me, but I think there is no labor greater than praying to God. For every time a man wants to pray, his enemies the demons try to prevent him; for they know that nothing obstructs them so much as prayer to God. In everything else that a man undertakes, if he perseveres, he will attain rest. But in order to pray a man must struggle to his last breath.[3]

God speaks to us in a variety of ways, including reading and reflecting—on scripture, His still small voice, our circumstances, and through our community; yet, most Christians have difficulty knowing what the Lord specifically wants of them. Hearing from God is the source of our calling.

Hearing from the Lord clearly will always be a struggle on this side of heaven. As disciples of Jesus Christ, we must learn perseverance and practice the art of hearing from God. We must be willing to struggle continuously for His will for our lives and be willing to lay down our own will. There is no greater image of this than when Jesus struggled in the Garden of Gethsemane to hear from the Father about His imminent crucifixion:

> He took Peter and the two sons of Zebedee along with him, and he began to be sorrowful and troubled. Then he said to them, "My soul is overwhelmed with sorrow to the point of death. Stay here and keep watch with me." Going a little farther, he fell with his face to the ground and prayed, "My Father, if it is possible, may this cup be taken from me. Yet not as I will, but as you will." Then he returned to his disciples and found them sleeping. "Couldn't you men keep watch with me for one hour?" he asked Peter. "Watch and pray so that you will not fall into temptation. The spirit is willing, but the flesh is weak." He went away a second time and prayed, "My Father, if it is not possible for this cup to be taken away unless I drink it, may your will be done." When he came back, he again found them sleeping, because their eyes were heavy. So he left them and went away once more and prayed the third time, saying the same thing. (Matthew 26:37–44)

Jesus struggled and wrestled mightily as He desired to hear clearly from God about the call on His life. He literally sweated blood in His efforts

---

3. Kallistos Ware, *The Orthodox Way* (New York: St. Vladimir's Press, 1986), 33.

to align His desires with God's will. He had learned to hear from the Father and was ultimately willing to say, "Your will be done" (v. 42). This is what getting clarity of calling entails.

Secondly, we need to be trained to distinguish His voice from all others. This takes time and practice and involves temptation. Upon His call into public ministry, even Jesus was tempted by the devil. He had to choose between listening to the voice of the enemy or the voice of God the Father. We will spend a lifetime doing the same as disciples of Christ.

How do you hear from God? Can you distinguish between the voice of God and the voice of the world, between the flesh and the devil? What rhythms in your life promote hearing from God? What is missing?

UNDERSTANDING CALLING AND WORK

Remember in the Garden of Eden God would call to Adam and Eve in the cool of the evening and walk and talk with them. He would give them work to do that was both meaningful and fruitful. A crucial point to remember is that work existed before the Fall; work is part of creation.

We are wired for meaningful and fruitful work, and that desire will never subside. The enemy tries hard to keep us from our calling. Some of his strategies include convincing us that work is "bad." The results of this tragedy are prevalent in our culture.

There is a belief that if you make enough money or win the lottery, you have won the game of life and no longer need to work. We see work as drudgery, as something to be avoided. We sing songs and joke about avoiding work. We rarely celebrate the gift of work.

This mindset is a twist on the reality of the fall. When Adam ate the fruit, the curse he received and passed down to us was that our work would involve struggle, that we would have to contend with thorns and thistles. The enemy takes this reality and manipulates us to despise not the thorns and thistles but to despise the work itself. The enemy knows that if he can create in us a negative attitude towards work, he can keep us from our calling.

Recently a painter friend of mine told me of how associates staged accidents at work in order to draw disability and stop working. Instead of seeing disability as something to be avoided, there is a subculture that views this as hitting the jackpot. They thought of work as the enemy, as something that was keeping them from enjoying life, and they did what they could to opt out of meaningful work.

Physician friends testify to the same phenomenon. They tell me of the increasing number of people who come to their office requesting their signature in order to qualify for disability. The physician knows that patients who engage in meaningful and fruitful work are more apt to heal or heal more quickly, yet the doctor is still tempted to "sign off" anyway out of a desire to appease rather than heal. In some cases, there is an injury that would make the patient's current work prohibitive leaving the physician with the difficult task of encouraging them to engage in other meaningful work instead of going on disability.

This fallacy that work is bad also works its way into the notion of retirement. It goes something like this: If you work hard enough and save enough, you can retire and never be forced to work again. We look forward to retirement when we can finally enjoy the good life of no work. The enemy would have you believe that the goal of hard work is that you do not have to work anymore. Interestingly, the latest study out of Oregon State University tells us that people are much more likely to die younger by retiring early.[4] This study supports the view that a life of leisure and playing all day, does not actually satisfy, sustain, or give meaning. Because of this, people who do not engage in meaningful work die early.

Retirement from a Christian perspective should mean that I have saved up enough so that I no longer need to be paid to work. Instead, I can fully give myself to the work that God has called me to do in this season. Regardless of age, we are wired by God from the beginning of creation to do the good works that God has prepared for us. (See Ephesians 4:12.)

Another ploy of the enemy is to separate us from the work God intends for us to do by getting us to do the wrong work. If we are doing work that the Lord is not calling us to do, the enemy can separate us from the life God desires for us. Such was the case for me when I went to medical school. Interestingly, when I was in medical school, I volunteered as a youth minister and read books on theology. During the period of time that the medical school shut down after the hurricane, we had no electricity. There were many times of silence and solitude. In my prayers, I discerned that God had not called me to medical school. I returned anyway, but within weeks I was eating lunch with classmates and discussing our dreams of doing what we

---

4. "Want to live a long life? Don't retire early." April 28, 2016, http://www.thehealthsite.com/news/want-to-live-a-long-life-dont-retire-early-ag0416/

really wanted to do after making enough money as doctors. I can remember at the table God's saying to me, "Do you really want to waste that much of your life doing something you are not called to do just to make money? Why not trust Me and start living in your calling now?"

Later that week, I met with the president of the medical school and asked for a year off to think about things. I will never forget his response: "Allen, I have known you for a long time, and I never thought you were called to be a doctor." When I told my roommate this story, he agreed. He did not think I was called to be a doctor either. In fact, nobody I spoke with thought I should be a doctor. How did I miss my calling so badly? Why did I almost end up spending years of my life chasing money when what I really wanted to do was what God created me to do?

The answer is obvious and all too common. I wanted money, respect, and a career. I thought I needed to ensure that I would have those things rather than trusting that my Father in Heaven would provide. Those goals were not evil in and of themselves, but I wanted them more than I wanted to do what my Father had created and called me to do.

Too many of us are stuck in ruts of doing the wrong work. We made little decisions and compromises along the way, and now we wonder why we are doing what we are doing? We feel unsatisfied and wonder if our work has any meaning at all. As time passes, we feel stuck in a job we hate.

The enemy lies to us to keep us from our calling by reinforcing the false dichotomy between the sacred and the secular. If the enemy can get humanity to think that the only meaningful work is religious work, church work, or social justice, he has effectively paralyzed most of the world. Certainly, people are called to these professions, but these are not inherently better than being a teacher, a landscaper, a factory worker, a real estate agent, or a physician.

Another ploy of the enemy is to tempt us to overwork. Even if we are doing the work that we are called to do, we can make work into an idol. We can enjoy the rush of being successful, being the man who gets things done, or the woman who always closes the deal. Work takes the place of God in giving us our identity. When we let work define who we are, we unconsciously trade our identity as sons and daughters of the Living God and become slaves to a profession. Once we have made that shift, the work becomes the god, a god who has no mercy. Work consumes us and our interpersonal relationships with spouse, children, family, and friends all suffer. We become more isolated and more addicted to work because work seems to provide a sense of meaning. We have no friends. We feel like no one knows us or appreciates us.

Then we move into burnout. Ultimately, we can never work hard or long enough to satisfy our desire for success and identity. At this stage people tend to have a crisis. They grow discontent. They may quit their job, have a moral breakdown, or chase after other things for meaning. When one gets to this stage, they have no joy. People do not enjoy being around them, and they become difficult.

Because there is no joy, people will be willing to exchange joy for pleasure. Pleasure comes from the outward circumstances in life whereas joy comes from the heart and lasts regardless of the circumstances. Without joy, some will medicate with alcohol, drugs, and physical pleasure to fill the void. The tragedy is that many of these people started living into their calling but let the work take precedence over the God who called them.

In the summertime, there is a TV show I like to watch called American Pickers. It's a pseudo-documentary about two guys who travel the country in search of old antiques, cars, motorcycles, and other memorabilia. I love watching the show, not because of any interest in the things they collect, but because I like watching people who love what they do. The star is Mike, and the joy he has digging through old garages and storage sheds to find rusty pieces of gold is a pleasure to watch. When you are fully living into your calling you have a sense of joy and meaning.

The most effective evangelists today are those who are following their calling in their work. If you live a life in accordance with your calling, you will be filled with a joy that will be a light in our world! People will recognize that you are different; and, they will wonder how you can be so full of joy doing the work you are doing. They will notice that you do not complain, blame others, or think that someone is holding you back. You will actually give them hope by the way you live. You will draw them closer to God, and they will want to know your secret. Living out your calling will change the lives of those around you.

(A deeper discussion of all these Habits and Rhythms mentioned can be found on the podcast at TheGoodSoil.us.)

YELLOW FLAGS OF CALLING

My grandmother was an excellent gardener. She was vigilant. She walked her garden every day and was intentional about looking for signs of disease.

She knew the "yellow flags" to look for and knew that her responsibility as the gardener was to identify them and address the threats before they killed the crop. She developed a sixth sense for what was going on in the garden. Walking through, she would notice things that I could not see and say, "I think I need to add some iron" or "check the tomatoes for caterpillars." She could see the warning signs before things went off the rails. She could make the adjustments, adjust the soil, and deal with the pests before the fruit of the garden was ruined.

As Christians we can learn from this by being aware of the yellow flags that would indicate a problem in the area of calling. I look for these signs in my own speech and behavior as well as in those I disciple. If these yellow flags are evident in those I disciple, I know I am dealing with a calling issue.

To clearly understand our calling requires us to confront our sins and weaknesses in much the same way as Moses, Isaiah, and Jeremiah. Our Biblical heroes had to confront their own issues as they sought clarity about what God was calling them to do. Moses had to deal with the fact that he tried to live out his calling in his own strength. Joseph had to confront his pride in his calling. Jeremiah had to confront his sense of inadequacy.

Consider the following "yellow flags." If we can identify these, we can deal with them before they turn us from God's plan and render us unfruitful.

Blaming

> If my boss would just let me . . .
>
> If my colleague would have done . . .
>
> If my spouse did not spend so much money . . .
>
> If my friends really cared . . .
>
> If I had a family that . . .
>
> You won't believe what John did to me . Which explains why I . . .

When people start blaming others or circumstances for their unhappiness, they have lost a sense of God's purposes for their lives. We can unconsciously fall into the trap of believing that others have caused us to live as we live, that others are responsible for our difficulties, or that if others changed, our lives would be better. Blaming others and blaming circumstances indicates a lack of clear vision. When you have a clear call from God you know that nothing can stop His call from being fulfilled.

Even our own sin or disobedience cannot remove us from our calling. God can restore the years the locusts have eaten. (See Joel 2:25.) Romans 8:31–39 tells us that nothing can separate us from God's love, from hearing His voice, from living out His plans. So, we need to check our own hearts for blame and listen for any signs of blame in others we are discipling.

Blame goes all the way back to the Fall of Adam and Eve in the Garden:

> And he said, "Who told you that you were naked? Have you eaten from the tree that I commanded you not to eat from?" The man said, "The woman you put here with me—she gave me some fruit from the tree, and I ate it." (Genesis 3:11–12)

Ever since the fall, we have been tempted by the same thought. If we can blame someone or something else for our shortcomings, we can be justified for not living in obedience to our calling.

Complaining

> "Allen, I have been working all my life as a lawyer, and I hate it. But I don't know what else I could do to make a living."

> "I feel like I'm just going through the motions of life without any real direction. I've done everything I can, but nothing seems to help."

> "I never dreamed I would be where I am today. I always thought I would get more out of life."

> "If I had more money or a different job, I would be happy."

When I hear complaining, I know there is a disconnect in understanding the fact that God can use all things for His plans and purposes (See Genesis 50). Though similar to blaming, complaining takes a step further. When we complain, we are not only blaming others, but we are also saying that God does not have the best plan for our lives, that His calling is insufficient, and that what He desires for us will not, in fact, give us abundant life or joy. In my personal coaching times, I occasionally hear this summed up as "my life is unbearable!"

Complaining stems from the belief that living out one's calling includes no suffering or hard times. Suffering is part of the plan. Suffering serves as the crucible in which we learn. For that reason, we are instructed to "give thanks in all circumstances; for this is God's will for you in Christ Jesus" (1 Thessalonians 5:18). Disciples learn the behavioral pattern of rejoicing in all things:

> Rejoice in the Lord always. I will say it again: Rejoice! Let your gentleness be evident to all. The Lord is near. Do not be anxious about anything, but in every situation, by prayer and petition, with thanksgiving, present your requests to God. And the peace of God, which transcends all understanding, will guard your hearts and your minds in Christ Jesus. (Philippians 4:4–7)

Victim Mentality

When a person uses victim language, you know they are not clear about the fact that God has a call on their lives, and they have a responsibility for this as well. Victims convey a sense that they are powerless over circumstances and that there is nothing they can do to change. In some sense this is true. We cannot control other people or many circumstances, but this thinking fails to acknowledge our part:

> What, then, shall we say in response to these things? If God is for us, who can be against us? No, in all these things we are more than conquerors through him who loved us. For I am convinced that neither death nor life, neither angels nor demons, neither the present nor the future, nor any powers, neither height nor depth, nor anything else in all creation, will be able to separate us from the love of God that is in Christ Jesus our Lord. (Romans 8:31, 37–39)

I am not making light of the victim mentality. Of course, all of us have, in some sense, been victims—victims of abuse, victims of abandonment, victims of crime, victims of racism, ad infinitum. However, as Christians we must understand and inwardly digest the truth of Christ's victory on the cross. We are not perpetually subject to victimhood.

Jesus was a victim of abuse, a victim of abandonment, a victim of crime, and a victim of persecution; yet, he was victorious over all—victorious over death, victorious over sin, victorious over identifying as a victim. In spite of what was done to Him in the past, Jesus is the King of kings and Lord of lords.

As Christians, we are like Him, and we too can throw off the victim mentality and live victorious lives. In fact, having the identity of a victim is almost a complete roadblock to one's ability to live into God's calling.

Overcoming the victim mentality is hard, serious work for many, and this aspect of discipleship has sometimes been lacking in the church. It is not simply a matter of verbally assenting to this truth. Victims often need the church to offer significant healing and restoration.

Regret

If I only could undo . . .

I wish I never . . .

There is no coming back from . . .

I messed up bad and there is no way to get back on track . . .

If people knew what I did or thought . . .

When we dwell on our past bad decisions, we fall into a serious trap because there is no way to undo the past. The mental energy we spend regretting things we have done can be paralyzing. Focusing on past mistakes gives them more power than necessary and hinders us from fulfilling our calling. A good friend of mine often reminds me of this truth when he says, "I have given up the hope for a better past."

We must believe God can redeem all things and restore the years the locusts have eaten (See Joel 2:25). There is a difference between repentance and regret. Repentance starts with sorrow and concludes with a turning away from the harmful behavior. Regret is a refusal to let go of past decisions or actions. Regret is not for Christians. When one lives in regret, it is a sure sign there is interior work to be done. Regret will forestall responding to and living in the calling.

Scripture implores us brothers and sisters with these words:

> Whatever is true, whatever is noble, whatever is right, whatever is pure, whatever is lovely, whatever is admirable—if anything is excellent or praiseworthy—think about such things. Whatever you have learned or received or heard from me, or seen in me—put it into practice. And the God of peace will be with you." (Philippians 4:8–9)

Paul wrote these words because he knew disciples of Jesus would be tempted to think about the things we messed up, the things we blew up, the things we regret—the things about our lives that are ugly, indecent, and embarrassing. Being a disciple is learning to repent—not regret—and then learning to focus on the larger truth about ourselves and our future.

Confusion or Being "Stuck"

I am stuck in a dead-end job . . .

I am stuck in this relationship or this marriage . . .

I am stuck with my poor finances . . .

I am stuck in my crappy life . . .

The experience of feeling "stuck" is common. Christian leadership coach Terry Walling reports in his book *Stuck* that many of his clients feel as though they are running the race but are caught in an endless loop of uncertainty. They want answers now, but none seem forthcoming. It is not uncommon for Christians to wrestle with an inability to hear from the Lord about what to do next, leaving them feeling stuck.[5]

While this is consistent with all accounts of the Christian life, feeling stuck is a yellow flag indicating a need for intentional time to revisit the details of one's calling. Often we head out with God to fulfill our calling, but we stray off the path, insert our agendas, and stop listening. The next thing you know, we feel we are out there alone.

It is time to stop and listen again to the guidance of our Lord for next steps. Too many people try to find the way back in their own strength, and even though they are active, they feel like they are spinning in circles. When we recognize that this season of feeling stuck is actually a time when God is realigning our wills with His will for our lives, we can see the light at the end of the tunnel.

5. Terry Walling, Stuck, (ChurchSmart Resources, 2008), 5.

Lack of Personal Ownership

> There is nothing I can do . . .
>
> I have tried it all and nothing works . . .
>
> All my efforts are fruitless . . .
>
> I give up . . .

When people forgo their personal responsibility in discipleship they flounder. We have an active role in discipleship and must choose to believe that we play a part in the process. We are not just puppets of a benevolent god. Discipleship requires training. A willingness to train is the fertile soil for understanding your calling.

Because discipleship is an intentional act, scripture reminds us that "we are each responsible for our own conduct" (Galatians 6:5 NLT). St. Augustine wrote, "Without God we cannot; without us, He will not." There is a part of free will that necessitates our choosing to partner with God. We partner with Him because He has the strength and power to enable us to live into our calling:

> For physical training is of some value, but godliness has value for all things, holding promise for both the present life and the life to come. This is a trustworthy saying that deserves full acceptance. That is why we labor and strive, because we have put our hope in the living God, who is the Savior of all people, and especially of those who believe. (1 Timothy 4:8–10)

When we do not accept the charge to train as disciples of Christ, we reject our part of the relationship. Jesus lets the rich young ruler walk away from the invitation to be a disciple. Relationship even with Jesus takes effort. Walking with Jesus will always reveal opportunities for us to choose to move toward Him.

Burnout

I can't keep doing what I'm doing . . .

I am burning the candle at both ends . . .

It never ends and I can't take it anymore . . .

What is the point . . .

Unfortunately, workaholism is growing in our society. Even in the Christian world we encounter this phenomenon way too often. People generally start out trying to do good work, and yet the curse of man from Genesis 3 weighs on us. We get too much of our identity and sense of purpose from what we are doing, and the burden of production grows heavier and heavier.

Moses was a great leader, but he, too, experienced burnout as he was leading God's people out of bondage into the promised land. Luckily his father-in-law observed his work pattern and advised him:

> What you are doing is not good. You and these people who come to you will only wear yourselves out. The work is too heavy for you; you cannot handle it alone. Listen now to me, and I will give you some advice, and may God be with you. (Exodus 18:17–18)

Catching ourselves and our brothers and sisters who are at various stages of burnout is critical in the life of discipleship. When I hear people talking about multiple callings or a calling that is too broad, I quickly question if they are working too much, are consumed with their work, or feel like the work is never ending.

Clarity of calling is the remedy to burnout. It gives us the filter for what we say yes to and what we say no to. Saying yes to every "good" thing is not the life of a disciple. Jesus said yes only to things that the Father asked Him to do, and He is our model.

Dallas Willard was once asked what was one word he thought best described Jesus. Amazingly, his response was "relaxed . . . Jesus did not take on burdens that were not His to carry. He did not rush around trying to accomplish more than the Father asked of Him. He lived out His calling with an easy yoke.[6]

---

6. (https://www.soulshepherding.org/dallas-willards-one-word-for-jesus/)

Apathy, and Lack of Life Direction

I just don't care anymore . . .

There is no point in doing . . .

Nothing makes a difference . . .

Whatever . . .

When a person gets so removed from his or her calling, one temptation is to do nothing. This rationalization results in a person who does little to no work and actually becomes a burden to the Christian community. Paul addressed this in his letter to the Thessalonians:

> In the name of the Lord Jesus Christ, we command you, brothers and sisters, to keep away from every believer who is idle and disruptive and does not live according to the teaching you received from us. For you yourselves know how you ought to follow our example. We were not idle when we were with you, nor did we eat anyone's food without paying for it. On the contrary, we worked night and day, laboring and toiling so that we would not be a burden to any of you. We did this, not because we do not have the right to such help, but in order to offer ourselves as a model for you to imitate. For even when we were with you, we gave you this rule: "The one who is unwilling to work shall not eat." (2 Thessalonians 3: 6–10)

In our Christian communities we need to recognize this tendency in ourselves and others. We need to lovingly address the issue to spur them on and not let them fall into self-pity and idleness. A common symptom in those in this condition is the tendency to medicate with pleasure. They are always seeking some enjoyment in life but never finding the satisfaction they desire.

Privatized Calling

It's none of your business . . .

This is between me and God . . .

I don't trust people with . . .

My faith is private . . .

When a Christian says their calling is private or secret or none of your business, that is a yellow flag. Discussing your calling with other Christians is one of the best ways to gain clarity, to refine your understanding, and to get helpful feedback. Often the difficulty is finding those healthy communities of people who are equipped and trained to help you discern and live out your calling.

As disciples of Christ we must pursue this community, and remember Paul's admonition to "continue to work out your salvation with fear and trembling, for it is God who works in you to will and to act in order to fulfill his good purpose" (Philippians 2:12–13).

In the body of Christ, Paul teaches us that some are called to be eyes, some to be ears, while others . . . (See 1 Corinthians12.) Paul knew that the willingness and ability to help each find their place in the body brings health to the whole. If someone isolates from the body, it harms the whole body. You never get clarity of your calling alone.

We have looked at some of the habits and rhythms that create fertile soil enabling us to hear from God and gain clarity on our calling. We have looked at the warning signs to help us realize when we are disconnected from a life in sync with our calling. Hopefully, after this chapter you'll want to dive more deeply into your calling. Discipleship's foundation is the ability to hear the voice of God and align our lives with His will for us. For more on this topic, we invite you to go to TheGoodSoil.us.

5

Using the Tools of Discipleship

As I MATURED AS a gardener, I became interested in gardening tools and ordered catalogues filled with pages of tools. Before long reality set in—I was in over my head. I did not understand the purpose of the tools pictured or how to judge what was the best tool for a specific job. When I called a friend, an expert gardener, and asked for help, he gave me three things to remember:

1. Most mistakes happen when we use the wrong tool for the job.

2. Most people learning how to use a tool, fall in love with that tool and try to use it for everything. You need to develop the ability to work with many tools.

3. Knowing how to use a tool means knowing its inherent limitations.

In the Church, we have had a similar experience in discipleship efforts. There are many tools available for Christian living—programs, books, teachings, conferences, spiritual disciplines, gift tests, personality tests, and retreats among others. Most Christians are not sure where to start. What should they be signing up for, reading, listening to, and attending now? How do these tools fit into their Christian walk, which ones should they use, and how should they use them?

Know that the programs, studies, small groups, etc . . . that your church offers are the tools being offered to you for your development as a disciple of Jesus. Effective discipleship uses these tools the right way at the right times.

What complicates the effective use of the Christian tools is that we all have had some bad experiences with particular tools and have even been hurt by them. We have been in a bad small group, or to a Bible study that was not very helpful. Nevertheless, tools are invaluable to the Christian life. Part of being a disciple is understanding which tools are available and best suited for the job. Once you understand what you are trying to build, you start to understand which tool is necessary. When we are in the right program or we are addressing the growth issue needed, we are exactly where God wants us.

USING THE WRONG TOOL

Churches offer a myriad of classes, retreats, events, services, groups etc. These are the tools of discipleship, but which one should I sign up for? How do I know? Who decides which is best for me in my current situation? All too often we realize the things we are doing are not actually helping us grow and mature as Christians.

I bought a diamond-bladed weeding hoe which was great for weeding without bending over. It worked great on the paths between the plants. Unfortunately, when I saw the weeds that were growing next to my plants, I thought I could use the same tool with the same effects. What I actually did was remove the weeds while cutting the vital roots of the vegetables as well. The roots were under the ground, out of sight, and out of mind. Although on the outside it looked like this was working, I was using the wrong tool! In the end, my plants were weak and unproductive. I learned the hard way that I needed to use a different tool for that job.

In discipleship there will be times when I need to work on my character and other times when I need to serve the outcast, lonely and afraid. There are still other times when I need to worship or to pray. To mature as disciples, we will need to use different tools at different times.

To improve discipleship, we need to understand what we are trying to accomplish and then determine what is the best tool to help us accomplish that task. We do not just sign up for a class or join a group without knowing the reason and purpose. Conversely, when we have clarity about the area in which we need to grow and mature, we can better figure out the "tool" that will help us flourish.

Also, we understand that different cultures, denominations, and traditions have different ways they speak about the discipleship process. For example, an Evangelical may say, "The Lord spoke to me in my quiet time." The Anglican says, "I encountered God today through the practice of *Lectio Divina*," and the Charismatic says, "God spoke to me today while I was reading scripture." All of them are talking about an important experience of Christian discipleship, namely that of hearing from God through the reading of scripture, but each one is using a different tool to aid in the process. Some tools will not work within your culture or denomination. Do not get caught up in what the "bad tools" are. Rather, focus on the ones helpful to you and your community.

OVERUSE OF A TOOL

I once belonged to a church where the recurring message (though not actually stated) was this: "The answer to your questions and the solution to your problem is to have better quiet times." Do not get me wrong. I love having a quiet time, but the answer to all Christian discipleship issues is not "just go have a quiet time." That tool was not working for me. Yet, because it was the only tool in their toolbox, the problem was me.

In far too many of our churches, there are so few tools used that inevitably the same tool is used repeatedly. The tools worked before so why should we think it will not work again and again? The leader of the church has not been trained to use other discipleship tools effectively, so he keeps working the same thing. It takes time, energy, and wisdom to expand the toolbox.

Jesus teaches us, "Therefore every teacher of the law who has become a disciple in the kingdom of heaven is like the owner of a house who brings out of his storeroom new treasures as well as old" (Matthew 13:52). There are very effective tools that have been used for centuries and continue to work today; however, there are also many new tools being developed that are effective in our changing culture.

The overuse of a tool is often born out of a successful experience. A person experiences some class, conference, or book that helps them in their faith journey. So, the next time they are in need of help, they go back to the same tools, the same experience as if it had infinitely repeatable results.

Moses fell in love with one tool, the staff. In Exodus 4 God calls Moses out of Midian to return to Egypt and free his people. When Moses objects, God says that He will send Moses to do this task with signs. God instructs Moses to throw down the staff and it turned into a serpent; he instructs

Moses to put his hand into his robe and it comes out with leprosy. When Moses picks up the serpent it turns back into a staff and when he returns his hand into his robe the leprosy disappears. Moses loved the staff part; he never repeated the hand into the robe bit. Let's assume he was not a big fan of having leprosy even for a few seconds.

Moses used the staff to show up Pharaoh, to turn the Nile into blood, to part the Red Sea, and to get water out of a rock. He raised it in the air to win battles against their enemy. This was one impressive tool. Moses loved this tool. Then one day in the wilderness, God asked Moses to speak to a rock so that fresh water would flow out of the rock to give drink to the parched Israelites (Numbers 20). Moses ignored God's request to speak to the rock, and struck the rock with his trusty tool, his staff. For this seemingly innocuous use of his tool Moses was forbidden to enter the promised land.

God needed Moses to rely on him rather than on the one tool he was comfortable with. When God led them in battle against Jericho, He wanted them to dance around the walls and blow trumpets. I can imagine Moses would have insisted on hitting the walls with his staff instead. When they were to cross the Jordan River to enter the promised land, God instructed them to simply put their feet in the river and the waters parted. Had Moses not been corrected and been allowed to lead the Israelites across the Jordan, he probably would have insisted on using his staff to part the water as he had done in the past.

Moses' story is the classic overuse of a tool story. The staff had been effective so many times before Moses slipped into relying on the tool instead of the Lord. He pulled out the staff instead of asking the Lord for direction.

Contrast this with the way Jesus heals. He does so in many different ways. Sometimes He touches, others time people touch Him; sometimes He uses dirt and spit, when other times He just speaks healing from a distance. I think Jesus knew that if He did anything the same way every time, we would just copy His outward motions. We would use the tools without consulting the Master Gardener.

One fact that helps curb the overuse of a tool is realizing that there is no perfect tool. Some fall short in their effectiveness while some fall short in theological correctness or consistency. Some tools simply will not be used by some traditions because of underlying or explicit theological positions. Some tools are used in narrow situations, and others have a broader range of effectiveness.

Some tools have been deemed ineffective because they have been overused, when actually, they have merely been used poorly. I cannot tell you how many times in the church tools are used without subsequent follow up or evaluation. Consequently, the tool does not work as hoped; the blame gets directed at the tool instead of questioning the competency of those using the tool. Unfortunately, good tools go unused because people have been inoculated against them from bad experiences or overuse.

MISUSE OF A TOOL

A few churches I have encountered have given up on small groups. When I asked them why, they replied, "They just don't work in our setting." When asked what they were hoping to get out of them, they responded, "We want small groups to be a place where people can be cared for, where people can learn from the Bible, where people can have deep friendships, where people can figure out their gifting, where people can serve together, where people can pray and be prayed for, where people can . . ."

No wonder they "didn't work." Small groups are great and certain ones can do some of those things but none of them can do all of those things. Putting that kind of weight on a small group will ensure that it will collapse under its own weight.

No tool can do all we need, and every tool was developed for a certain task. Too often in discipleship there is a growing ignorance of the tools and why they were developed. Additionally, the expectations and limitations of the tool are not openly discussed or understood. We need to be able to explain the tools and what we expect out of them.

For example, "The Myers-Briggs Type Indicator" is a personality test. It may not be the best one, but it is one that is widely used and generally understood. It is very broad in the sense that it puts everyone into one of sixteen categories.

Other personality tests may be more specific and can expose deeper truths, but the Myers-Briggs tool is helpful to a certain extent. It is quick and easy to understand. It creates a common language that is helpful for understanding yourself, your family members, your co-workers, and others whose lives closely impact yours.

When my wife and I read each other's Myers-Briggs results and realized that I was an extrovert that gets energized in a completely different way from my introverted wife, we understood each other better. We were able to make better decisions about how we spent our time, and our marriage improved. However, we have not based our marriage and life on this one personality test. Though it is a helpful tool, it has limitations.

IN CLOSING

The church loves tools. We love the programs, the classes, the great teachings, the powerful worship, etc. But, we would do well to stop and ask questions before we add or sign up for something else at church. Where are we in the maturing of our faith and what tool/program is best designed to help us grow in that area? What discipleship deficiencies are we experiencing? What are our current tools and are we using them effectively? What discipleship needs are the current programs addressing well and what are we missing? What are my goals for maturing as a disciple and what are the tools needed for that job?

Please visit the website TheGoodSoil.us where we discuss more about the "tools" of discipleship.

6

The Good Soil of Equipping

ONGOING CYCLE OF DISCIPLESHIP

Calling
"Hearing God"

Community
"The Body of Christ"

Ministry
"The good works called to do"

Equipping
"Character and gifting"

ONCE WE HAVE A clear sense of what God is calling us to do, we have a tendency to jump straight into action. This chapter is about the importance of being equipped before we act. It is about the humility which acknowledges that we cannot do the things God is calling us to do alone. It is about the need to develop habits of examining our character. It is an admission that we are broken vessels and are in need of healing.

Trevor is a friend of mine. He is in his seventies and is active and fit. He takes lengthy hikes, repels off cliffs, climbs mountains, rafts rivers, and kayaks in the ocean. But this is not what impresses me about him. What I admire most about him is that he is fruitful in his ministry, men love to be around him, and he leads and disciples them beautifully.

In getting to know Trevor, I realized he had a true sense of calling from the Lord. But I have met many who have a similar call on their lives with much less fruit. I asked him what he was doing to be so fruitful. I watched him in action and made mental notes of his ministry style. I asked those to whom he ministered what drew them to him.

What I learned through my investigation was that Trevor has been training for his ministry for over fifty years and that he has continually sought equipping. He has been identifying his gifts and working on them for decades. He has been gaining clarity on his personality and wiring and has a humble self-awareness. He has dealt with pain and wounding in his life, has received healing, and can give testimony to you.

His character has been shaped through the many crucibles of life: friends who betrayed him, ministers who falsely accused him, and a wife who died way too young, to name a few. Through all this, he does not think he has arrived. Grown, yes, but he continues to seek the equipping of God as if he still has much to learn and much living ahead of him. Trevor is a man of God who understands the ongoing and life-giving nature of God's equipping. He seeks to learn instead of acting like he has arrived.

So, let's look at the principle of equipping through the lens of scripture.

BIBLICAL UNDERSTANDING OF EQUIPPING

Once the Lord has called you, He always equips you for the work He has called you to do. (See 1 Corinthians 12, Romans 12.). King David was said to lead with both integrity of heart and skillful hands. (See Psalm 78:72.) This description of King David gives us insight into the complex nature of equipping. Equipping involves both "being" and "doing."

Equipping includes:

- The receiving, discerning, and stewardship of gifts
- Ongoing character development

- Identifying the areas of healing we need
- Commitment to soul care
- A growing humble self-awareness

Scripture paints a clear picture that the life of a disciple includes growth, training, and maturity. Discipleship is possible when we realize that we do not have it all together. We do not have all the answers, and we do not know what to do. Nevertheless, we are following the One who will use us, train us in the ways we need to walk, and equip us for every good work we are asked to do.

Joseph and Equipping

As a teenager, Joseph heard a call from the Lord through two powerful and rich dreams involving his father and brothers bowing to him. What Joseph did not fully realize was that his calling was to be an effective administrator so that he would steward resources to bless others. Joseph was immature. He had not been equipped. He lacked the skills to interpret the dream or the wisdom to know what to do with the information. Consequently, he unwisely shared the dreams with his brothers. The details of the dreams gave the impression that Joseph would rule over them. Offended by those implications, his brothers devised a plan to kill him and ended by selling him into slavery.

Joseph wound up in the home of Potiphar, one of Pharaoh's officials. Recognizing Joseph's gifts, Potiphar promoted him to overseer and placed his household and all his possessions under the young man's authority. During those years, God was equipping him for his calling to administer and steward greater resources for the benefit of many. Unfortunately for Joseph, Potiphar's wife took notice of the handsome overseer and began to solicit his attention. When he rejected her sexual advances, she responded in rage and humiliation by falsely accusing him of rape. Potiphar threw Joseph into Pharaoh's prison, where he was again forced to face his lack of control over his circumstances. Thus, another season of character development had begun for the young man.

During Joseph's imprisonment, God was at work equipping him in terms of both doing and being. Joseph found favor with the warden and was placed in charge of the prison, another opportunity to hone his administrative gifts. He was also growing in character and humility. He met two officials in prison—a cupbearer and a baker who had each had a dream. God gave Joseph the ability to interpret their dreams, and his interpretations proved to be accurate. The cupbearer was restored and released from jail. Joseph's one request was that the cupbearer would remember him and let the authorities know.

Joseph was obviously hoping to get out of jail. Unfortunately, the cupbearer promptly forgot Joseph, and two years passed with no word of release for him. Joseph was learning patience; he was learning about God's timing, and he was learning that the Lord is the source of all good things.

Then in a seminal moment, we see him before Pharaoh being asked to interpret a dream:

> Pharaoh said to Joseph, "I had a dream, and no one can interpret it. But I have heard it said of you that when you hear a dream you can interpret it." "I cannot do it," Joseph replied to Pharaoh, "but God will give Pharaoh the answer he desires." (Genesis 41:15–16)

Notice the maturing from his teen years to adulthood, from boldly sharing his dreams indicating future authority over his brothers, to his humble response to Pharaoh that he could not interpret the dream, but God could. God was preparing him both in "being" and "doing" for this moment in his ministry. He had developed the humility of knowing where the power came from and the confidence in God's equipping and anointing of him to serve as administrator over all Egypt. His character, his gift for interpreting dreams, and his gifts of administration had matured. At that point, he was ready in terms of character and preparation for his calling. The result? He gained the trust of Pharaoh and was given authority over all Egypt.

Moses and Equipping

We see a similar experience with Moses. God worked through circumstances to have Moses raised from infancy in the house of Pharaoh. During this time, he learned to lead, govern, and guide. As he began to get clarity on his calling to help free his enslaved and abused people, he reacted rashly. In his desire to help the Israelites, he actually killed an Egyptian.

Moses's plans were now shot. He had to flee Egypt due to his actions. At this point, it may have seemed to Moses that all his preparation had been for nothing. He moved to the outskirts of society and spent forty years in

Midian. Moses may have had leadership gifts, but God still needed to work on his character. Moses needed to develop patience and humility.

After forty years, God renewed the call on Moses to free his people from the bondage of Egypt and lead them to the Promised Land. When He spoke to Moses through a burning bush, Moses was able to respond with humility, "Who am I that I should go to Pharaoh and bring the Israelites out of Egypt?" (Exodus 3:11).

Moses spent forty years being equipped through the patience and humility that comes from goat herding in the wilderness. God needed to equip Moses before Moses could be released to set the people free. The Lord knew of the challenges and hardships they would face on their journey through the desert into the Promised Land. God knew what amount of patience, humility, and reliance on Him would be required for the task. Once Moses was properly equipped, God released him to live in fulfillment of his calling.

David and Equipping

In Psalm 78:72, we read that David ruled or shepherded his people with "integrity of heart" and "skillful hands." David was a man after God's heart. When God sent Samuel to Jesse's house to anoint the next king of Israel, He corrected Samuel's assumption based on worldly criteria that Eliab must be the one:

> Do not consider his appearance or his height, for I have rejected him. The Lord does not look at the things people look at. People look at the outward appearance, but the Lord looks at the heart. (1 Samuel 16:7)

Instead, of the eight sons of Jesse, the Lord directed Samuel to the youngest who was given the humble work of tending the flocks. The Lord's equipping of David began with David's work in the fields. As shepherd, he learned to protect the flock from thieves and wild animals. He learned to stand against evil intended for the flock. His humble origins as the youngest of eight sons and shepherd of his father's flocks prepared David to shepherd God's people as king—the greatest king of Israel.

David's heart had also been equipped for his calling to become king. David had been equipped to trust the Lord and to understand his unique equipping. When Goliath and the Philistines were insulting and threatening the Israelites, the men cowered in fear; yet, David said to King Saul:

> "Let no one lose heart on account of this Philistine; your servant will go and fight him." Saul replied, "You are not able to go out against this Philistine and fight him; you are only a young man, and he has been a warrior from his youth." But David said to Saul, "Your servant has been keeping his father's sheep. When a lion or a bear came and carried off a sheep from the flock, I went after it, struck it and rescued the sheep from its mouth. When it turned on me, I seized it by its hair, struck it and killed it. Your servant has killed both the lion and the bear; this uncircumcised Philistine will be like one of them, because he has defied the armies of the living God. The Lord who rescued me from the paw of the lion and the paw of the bear will rescue me from the hand of this Philistine." (1 Samuel 17:32–37)

David's comments show us he understood that his equipping as a shepherd was preparation for this new calling. He had learned to rescue the sheep from assault. He knew how to fight a more powerful enemy, and he had developed a heart that trusted the Lord for the victory.

David defeated the giant and was clearly called to be king; but, his equipping was not over. King Saul turned against David and forced him into exile. In exile, he learned how to care for the men who served him—when to be tough, when to inspire, when to stand and fight and when to live to fight another day. David trained mighty men, loved them, and modeled a humble and gracious attitude towards the Lord. While hiding in a cave from the Philistine army at Bethlehem, three of David's mighty men heard of David's thirst and risked their lives to retrieve water for their leader. However, David refused to consider himself worthy of such a precious risk and instead of drinking it, he poured the water out as an offering before the Lord. "Far be it from me, Lord, to do this!" he said. "Is it not the blood of men who went at the risk of their lives?" (2 Samuel 23:17).

David modeled respect for his men and respect for the Lord. Their actions were honored in the greatest fashion by the water's becoming a drink offering for the Lord. David was called and equipped by God to become a great king.

Jesus was Equipped

Jesus was called and equipped by God. Scriptures tells us that He emptied Himself, taking on the form of man. He had the humility to be human, to go through the process of learning, remembering, and being fathered in all things. He had to study scripture. He memorized scripture. As a boy His parents found Him in the temple courts, sitting among the teachers, listening to them and asking them questions. (See Luke 2:46.)

Jesus was the perfect model for humanity. He spent the first thirty years of life learning and being equipped for the work He was called to do. He was so thoroughly equipped that when He was in the Garden of Gethsemane, He could honestly pray, "My Father, if it is possible, may this cup be taken from me. Yet not as I will, but as you will" (Matthew 26:39b).

Jesus Equips His Disciples

When we look at the life of Jesus and His methods of discipleship, we see that He discipled through an incarnational presence with those He was discipling. He was with them in the flesh. He was intentional about training them. He modeled ministry for them. He constantly taught them. He then kept giving them the opportunity to go out and do ministry.

He was also very concerned with their hearts. Jesus was intentionally spending three years to train, equip, and develop the character of the twelve so that they would be equipped to build the church after He was gone. He knew character mattered. His critique of the Jewish religious leaders was that they might have been educated in theology, but their hearts were far from God. (See Matthew 15:8.) Jesus' plan for discipleship included character development and humility as well as training in doing ministry.

Jesus Models

In Matthew 4:19, Jesus initiates the calling of His disciples with the charge, "Follow me, and I will make you fishers of men" (ESV). It is safe to assume that these men knew what it took to become good fishermen. They spent many years learning from their fathers, their relatives, and others whom they trusted in the village. They were taught to tie knots, mend nets, sail boats, repair leaks, and prepare fish. They had memories of past failures and of learning how to improve from the more experienced fishermen. They knew that they were not born being good fisherman but that the craft was learned through effort, training, mentoring, and experience.

They also knew that being a good fisherman was not limited to knowledge and technique but also required character. They were taught how to be patient and persevere when the fishing was bad. They were taught how to respect other fishermen and not cause undue adversity when they were doing well, and others were struggling. They were taught such fishing "etiquette" as not fishing a spot already being fished. They knew that success in fishing required hard work, diligence, and character.

Framing the invitation in terms of the craft that had been a life-long, learning process for them gave the disciples an image of what was being asked of them. The invitation was compelling, but also one they knew would require training and equipping for success in an adventure that was more than any they had experienced. Jesus knew that they would not be good at it at first. They would have failures, they would be challenged, and they would require hands-on instruction from Him. So, when we look at the life of Jesus and His disciples this is exactly what we see—Jesus modeled fishing for men. He taught by word and example and corrected them when they were off base, all the while shining a light on their character issues.

Jesus Instructs

When Jesus sent out the Twelve, He gave a long list of instructions:

> "Do not go among the Gentiles or enter any town of the Samaritans. Go rather to the lost sheep of Israel. As you go, proclaim this message: 'The kingdom of heaven has come near.' Heal the sick, raise the dead, cleanse those who have leprosy, drive out demons. Freely you have received; freely give. Do not get any gold or silver or copper to take with you in your belts—no bag for the journey or extra shirt or sandals or a staff, for the worker is worth his keep. Whatever town or village you enter, search there for some worthy person and stay at their house until you leave. As you enter the home, give it your greeting. If the home is deserving, let your peace rest on it; if it is not, let your peace return to you. If anyone will not welcome you or listen to your words, leave that home or town and shake the dust off your feet. Truly I tell you, it will be more bearable for Sodom and Gomorrah on the day of judgment than for that town, I am sending you out like sheep among wolves. Therefore be as shrewd as snakes and as innocent as doves. Be on

your guard; you will be handed over to the local councils and be flogged in the synagogues. On my account you will be brought before governors and kings as witnesses to them and to the Gentiles. But when they arrest you, do not worry about what to say or how to say it. At that time you will be given what to say, for it will not be you speaking, but the Spirit of your Father speaking through you." (Matthew 10:5–20)

Jesus was preparing them for the task of being disciples. He was teaching generosity, trust in Him for provision, time management, discernment, how to deal with difficult circumstances, enduring perseverance, and relying on the Spirit.

Later when Jesus sent out the seventy-two, He gave instruction about spiritual warfare. (See Luke 10:1–24.) He taught them how to work the harvest, how to manage finances, and when to stay in certain ministries and when to walk away. Jesus was always equipping and training His disciples before He sent them out to work. When they returned, they always had both testimony and questions. They had had success and they also had learned more of what they did not know about their ministry.

Jesus Asks and Answers Questions

In response to challenging teachings on discipleship, His followers questioned who could accept such teachings. When Jesus asked if they were offended, many walked away. With a well-timed question, Jesus gave the disciples opportunity to weigh His words and consider the cost of discipleship—both the cost of following and the cost of walking away.

Aware that His disciples were grumbling about this, Jesus said to them, "Does this offend you? Then what if you see the Son of Man ascend to where he was before! The Spirit gives life; the flesh counts for nothing. The words I have spoken to you—-they are full of the Spirit and life. Yet there are some of you who do not believe." For Jesus had known from the beginning which of them did not believe and who would betray him. He went on to say, "This is why I told you that no one can come to me unless the Father has enabled them." (John 6:61–65)

When Jesus asked the Twelve if they too wanted to leave, Peter responded, "Lord, to whom shall we go? You have the words of eternal life.

We have come to believe and to know that you are the Holy One of God"
(John 6:68–69).

Jesus knew the art of asking good questions in His equipping of His
disciples. He knew that questions often do a better job of revealing what is
in our hearts than making statements. Jesus understood that asking questions and allowing time for processing is critical in the equipping of the
saints for ministry.

On another occasion, Jesus was able to heal a boy after the disciples
had tried and failed. Having watched what Jesus did, they waited for a
time in private with Him to ask, "Why couldn't we drive it out?" (Matthew
17:19b). This was the right question and they were asking the right person.
Often our equipping comes from failures that hopefully turn into questions
for the Lord. Discipleship is not a performance but a journey of failures and
successes all of which drive us closer to Him. That gives us reason to turn
to Him and ask questions so that we can become more fully equipped to do
the work we are called to do.

Jesus Addresses Character

In Luke 9:51–55, Jesus instructed His disciples to go ahead of Him and
prepare for their arrival in a nearby village. When that village rejected Him,
His two right-hand men, James and John, having just come down from the
Mount of Transfiguration and knowing that Jesus was divine, asked Him,
"Lord, do you want us to tell fire to come down from heaven and consume
them?" (v. 54 ESV). Jesus immediately turned to them and rebuked them.
He saw the judgment growing in their hearts and knew He could not use
men like that to build His kingdom. He took the time then to correct them
and have them reflect on God's ways. Character matters!

In Mark 10, James and John again came to Jesus aware that He was
heading towards His death and glory. They boldly requested, "Grant us to
sit, one at your right hand and one at your left, in your glory" (v. 37 ESV).
Again, Jesus took time to equip them and help them understand the character of a disciple. He took the time to teach them of the coming Kingdom
of God. He explained that His disciples will not lord it over others from
places of high position but rather will serve those to whom they are sent.
Jesus explained that in the coming Kingdom the greatest leader will serve
and become like a slave. Yet, again Jesus was willing to take the time to let

these men develop the character they would need to lead the church when He was gone. Pride is the enemy of godly character.

In Matthew 16, Jesus asked Peter who he thought Jesus was. Peter with all his bravado proclaimed that Jesus was the Christ, the salvation of the world. Jesus affirmed the accuracy of Peter's response. We think Peter must be a great disciple. But then, right after this grand moment, Jesus explained that he was going to Jerusalem to be handed over to the religious leaders and killed. Peter adamantly rejected this idea and said that it would never happen. Jesus replied, "Get behind me, Satan! You are a hindrance to me. For you are not setting your mind on the things of God, but on the things of man" (v. 23 ESV). Peter had great faith and leadership ability, but Jesus knew Peter needed more character development. He needed to be aware of his tendency to contradict the Lord when he could not understand. Jesus was teaching Peter that he still had a tendency to see with worldly eyes and expectations; whereas, what was needed of him was to have a godly perspective. Even in the most difficult times for Jesus, He took the time to work on His disciples' character.

Jesus had already affirmed Peter as the chosen leader of His church, but notice, He did not avoid having the hard conversation about Peter's ongoing desire to have things done his way instead of listening to the Father and doing things God's way. Jesus will continuously call us to grow in character if we have ears to hear what He is saying.

Equipping in the Letters

As we look at the epistles, we see instruction and encouragement for maturing in faith, character development and practicing the skill of discipleship.

Maturing

The Apostle Paul emphasizes the importance of maturing in faith in his address to the church in Corinth: When I was a child, I spoke like a child, I thought like a child, I reasoned like a child. When I became a man, I gave up childish ways (1 Corinthians 13:11 ESV). Again, Paul points to a lack of maturity in the faith as he addressed the problems in the church in Ephesus:

> And He gave the apostles, the prophets, the evangelists, the shepherds and teachers to equip the saints for the work of ministry,

for building up the body of Christ, until we all attain to the unity of the faith and of the knowledge of the Son of God, to mature manhood, to the measure of the stature of the fullness of Christ, so that we may no longer be children, tossed to and fro by the waves and carried about by every wind of doctrine, by human cunning, by craftiness in deceitful schemes. Rather, speaking the truth in love, we are to grow up in every way into him who is the head, into Christ. (Ephesians 4:11–15 ESV)

And again in Hebrews Paul urges the church to persevere in maturing:

For though by this time you ought to be teachers, you need someone to teach you again the basic principles of the oracles of God. You need milk, not solid food, for everyone who lives on milk is unskilled in the word of righteousness, since he is a child . . . Therefore let us leave the elementary doctrine of Christ and go on to maturity . . . (Hebrews 5:12–13, 6:1 ESV)

Training

The epistles underscore the need for all disciples to train in the ways of the Lord. The Lord wants us to grow, and He knows that this takes effort. Paul encouraged the church to train for their faith as an athlete trains for his sport: "Everyone who competes in the games goes into strict training. They do it to get a crown that will not last, but we do it to get a crown that will last forever" (1 Corinthians 9:24). Later Paul instructed his disciple Timothy to train in righteousness:

Have nothing to do with godless myths and old wives' tales; rather, train yourself to be godly. For physical training is of some value, but godliness has value for all things, holding promise for both the present life and the life to come. This is a trustworthy saying that deserves full acceptance. That is why we labor and strive, because we have put our hope in the living God, who is the Savior of all people, and especially of those who believe. (1 Timothy 4:7–10)

The Apostle Paul understood that discipleship involved maturing and training. His calling was to encourage the Christians in the church to do the hard work of equipping and enjoy participating in the work of building God's Kingdom. Maturing in character and in proficiency is a life-long process for all disciples.

Clearly the Bible shows us that one of the ways God loves us is by equipping us to do the work He has given us to do. Going forward, let us look at what habits and rhythms we can build into our lives so that we do not miss out on the crucial element of discipleship that creates the good soil.

7

Working the Soil of Equipping

IN THIS CHAPTER, WE will look at the habits and rhythms of the disciples who seek and allow God to equip them for ministry. These are the overarching principles that guide all healthy training programs. When understood, they will help us follow a life-giving plan that will lead to our maturing as disciples of Jesus.

As a new convert in high school, I was pressured to speak to students about God and divorce. Why me? Well, as the only one on the team whose parents were divorced, the honor fell to me. I honestly cannot remember a single word of that talk. It would have been a miracle of God if anything I said was used to draw others close to Him. Although I was called to teach, I had a fear of public speaking and no experience, training, or equipping in teaching. I had no grounding in my faith, no healing from the divorce, and I was in need of character growth. I was the perfect choice. I failed miserably.

What I experienced is a common mistake in the church. The church saw a need and filled it with someone before equipping them. Can you imagine if Jesus spent a weekend with the disciples and then set them loose on the world? Think of what the twelve would have done without training? I can imagine Judas would have recommended a lucrative plan of ministry. James and John would have fought to be in charge. Peter would have gone off by himself half-cocked. They would have called down hellfire on those who didn't listen. I believe the whole thing would have exploded in failure.

INTENTIONALITY

Knowing the maturity level of His disciples, Jesus spent three years living with them—teaching, modeling, training, equipping, answering questions, healing them, and developing their character. Moreover, He was allowing them to process what the kingdom of God was all about as well as what their role would be in advancing His Kingdom.

The military has clear structures in place to train soldiers. First they equip; then they deploy. They do not send untrained soldiers to do work that often has life or death outcomes. Secondly, they continue to equip and train soldiers throughout their career. Training in the military is never over but constantly progresses to the next level. Thirdly, soldiers who move up the ranks train and equip others. Advancing in leadership results in increased responsibility for the training of others. Finally, everyone in the military realizes character matters—soldiers obey orders or go to jail. Soldiers have each other's back, or all morale is lost. Actions matter whether or not others are looking.

Additionally, every successful military has rhythms of training, deployment, and rest. Soldiers need a schedule that reflects a balance of the three. Soldiers must be properly trained to perform well. Before being deployed soldiers need to be equipped, rested, and supported. And, soldiers need rest after a season of deployment.

The military starts with the end in mind—victory in battle—and then creates the healthy rhythms and structures that make that victory most possible. As Christians, we all want to be fruitful in our ministry and to be a part of others' being transformed in response to the Gospel of Jesus Christ. With this in mind, we must ask what rhythms and habits will best prepare us to be victorious in our efforts. What are the habits of Christians who are committed to being equipped?

BALANCE OF DOING AND BEING

In the fictional book *Joshua* by Joseph Girzone[1] there is a modern-day Jesus character who is a carpenter. He makes wooden statues. Two pastors ask him to make a statue of Peter. The small church pastor wants a statue that shows Peter's humility. His church is small and struggles along. He wants to comfort his people with a statue that depicts the humility and lowliness that

1. Joseph Grizone, Joshua: A Parable for Today, New York: Doubleday, 1994.

Jesus took on as a man. The large church pastor wants a representation of Peter's boldness and fire. His church is large, and he is always encouraging his congregation to greater heights and boldness.

When they come to pick up their statues, they are amazed at how well the statues depict the side of Peter they admire. However, when Joshua hands them their statues, he gives each the one that the other pastor wanted. The inference is that Jesus wants to remind them of the things they are not, the things they avoid, the part of the faith they tend to ignore. I find this true as Christians try to balance being and doing.

I definitely lean on the doing side. I love to learn and want to get better in so many areas of my gifting. I want to act, to go, to participate in all that God has for me. I am not patient. I need healing in so many areas of my heart and have character flaws; but, if it were up to me, I would just press on and ignore these things.

In contrast, my friend Billy loves to contemplate the love of God, participate in silent retreats, and take time to dwell in God's presence; but He is not clear on his gifting and tends to wait too long before he acts.

We both need balance, and we need others to help us with this. Both are important. We do not want to do ministry with a lack of character. This will inevitably lead to a moral failure. People will see through us and not be drawn to God because of our lack of character. We also do not want to work on ourselves alone and never do anything for others. We will become self-absorbed, self-focused, and ultimately no good for the growth of the Kingdom. We all tend to lean one way or the other. Do you prefer working on your character or your gifting? Do people say you love to be with God or that you do lots for God?

God is at work in your life building both skillful hands and integrity of heart. He is preparing you to do good works in His name. He is always at work. We often seek training and are intentional about getting the discipleship we need to grow and be effective. What we frequently forget is that when we are not intentional about being equipped, God is equipping us anyway. He is doing that right now in our lives. He is doing it whether we know it or not. He will use every incident, every tragedy, and every circumstance for His good purposes. Training is not really something we can opt out of, so why not seek it out within the healthy confines of Christian community?

Where are you in the spectrum of doing for God and being with God? Do you do too much? Do you do too little? What do you think God is asking of you in this season of life—to focus more on what you are doing or who you are in Him? How do you keep the balance? What do others say about you in this area of life?

LIFE-LONG LEARNING AND MATURING

There are myriads of new studies out that tell us basically the same thing. Ongoing learning is good for your memory and brain. We are created to learn. When we stop, we start to die. Being a disciple of Jesus is a commitment to life-long learning.

We need to create an expectation that we will always be on a journey of growth. We need to commit to ongoing learning about God and our faith, ongoing training in our calling, ongoing growth in maturity, and ongoing character development.

My coach Terry is an older man and has trained and equipped me in multiple areas of my faith. I respect and love him for his investment in my discipleship. However, the thing about Terry that most surprises me as my mentor is that he is learning from me. I should be clear, I have learned much more from him, but as he disciples me, he is learning from me, as well, and readily admits it. He reminds me that as Christians we are never done growing as we work out our salvation with fear and trembling.

The Apostle Peter was not fully equipped the week after he met Jesus. Even after three years with Jesus, he had not learned everything. He was not fully trained after the resurrection, and he was not fully equipped after Pentecost. When his character needed to be worked on, God had Paul confront him at the council of Jerusalem about his attitude toward the Gentiles.

What are you learning now? How do you decide what you want to learn? What do others around you encourage you to learn about? What rhythms in your life promote healthy learning?

HUMBLE SELF AWARENESS

"A humble self knowledge is a surer way to God than a search after deeper learning."[2] (Thomas à Kempis)

2. Thomas à Kempis, *The Imitation of Christ* [Book 1, Chapter 4]

When I called Mark because he was an expert in church planting, I asked him a lot of questions. His response surprised me: "I do not know, that is not my area of expertise. I focus on planting in big cities. I don't feel comfortable giving advice on church planting in suburban environments or small towns."

At first, I was shocked by his reply. I fully expected him to extrapolate his success in every area of life, and I wanted him to do so. Most of the people I talk to want to come across as experts or at least as very knowledgeable. He had great answers to many questions and was willing to share his insight. However, he was also careful not to speak on things he did not really know. He had a humble self-awareness. He knew what he had to offer and what his limitations were. In an image-driven world where everyone is putting their best foot forward on social media and being encouraged to brand themselves, humility is having a hard time claiming its rightful place in our lives—namely at the very center.

Humility is the key to unlocking our identity as Christians. First and foremost, we realize that we all fall short of who we were intended to be; we all have turned our backs on our Creator and tried to take His rightful place; and, we have all missed the mark and stand on equal footing before the cross in need of a savior. It is then and only then that we should look at the *imago dei* that is still intact. We have been made in God's image, and we have not lost all of that. Furthermore, God continues to redeem us, sanctify us, and give us gifts to accomplish the work He has called us to do.

This kind of self-awareness starts in humility and guides us to examine our unique nature, gifting, personality, passions and desires in a way that glorifies God and allows us to participate in the ushering in of His Kingdom. Christians do not believe we are all just cogs in a machine. Rather, as adopted sons and daughters, we have unique roles and gift mixes that God desires for us to use every day.

Do you know who you are in the Lord? Do you start with the humility of a fallen human? Do you realize He is calling you up to be a son or daughter of the King? What is your personality? Your gifting? Do you feel comfortable in your own skin?

SCRIPTURE READING

Christian history details a long list of men and women who sacrificed and even died so that people had access to scripture. To engage in healthy rhythms of reading scripture, praying scripture, and meditating on scripture is essential to discipleship. Even though we understand the need for these rhythms, I would argue that the urgency evades the majority of Christians today.

To be a disciple without this habit is like driving with both hands tied behind your back; it is foolish and dangerous to others. Jesus knew that "all Scripture is God-breathed and is useful for teaching, rebuking, correcting and training in righteousness, so that the servant of God may be thoroughly equipped for every good work" (2 Timothy 3:16–17). This is why Jesus dedicated Himself to the study, memorization, and application of scripture in daily life.

In this present age where a multitude of world views compete for our allegiance, the habit of reading, listening to, and reflecting on scripture is what gives us perspective. As disciples, reading scripture will protect us from thought patterns that draw us away from God. Reading scripture will help us discern the voice of God from all the other voices clamoring for our attention. And, reading scripture will ground us in the life, death, and teachings of Jesus Christ.

What are your habits of reading and listening to scripture? Do you do it with others or always alone? Do you have a sense that you are very familiar with the main story of scripture? Does scripture guide your thoughts and decisions?

CHARACTER DEVELOPMENT

If we learn anything from Jesus' words in the Sermon on the Mount to "be perfect, therefore, as your heavenly Father is perfect" (Matthew 5:48), it should be that we all fall short. Jesus points out that even if our behavior is within the law, our hearts are far from pure. Since we all have character flaws, we are in need of character development as part of our training and discipleship. In addition, we all experience suffering which provides opportunity for character growth: "We also glory in our sufferings, because we know that suffering produces perseverance; perseverance, character; and character, hope" (Romans 5:3b–4).

During my time in seminary, I asked the Lord what was next for me and clearly heard in prayer, "I want you to return everything you have stolen." Now in my mind as a seminarian, I did not consider myself a thief. However, upon reflection, the Lord reminded me of things I had taken from my parents as a child and signs that I had relocated to my college dorm for decoration. He reminded me of the many things I had "borrowed" from family, friends and neighbors that never made it back to their possession.

To take matters further, He reminded me of things I wanted in my heart that I was not willing to pay for. I walked through weeks of returning and (to the extent that I could) replacing things, the most entertaining of which was the phone call to the local government about where to send money for new signs.

Jesus' disciples were no different. They argued over who got to be first in the Kingdom only to be taught that the first would be last in His kingdom. They were rebuked by Jesus for not being able to stay up for one hour and pray with Him. They were rebuked for wanting to destroy those who refused to listen to them. Because of His great love for the disciples, Jesus developed their character as He discipled them.

In 2 Peter 1:5b–9, we have a vivid description of the active nature and depth of character development:

> Make every effort to add to your faith goodness; and to goodness, knowledge; and to knowledge, self-control; and to self-control, perseverance; and to perseverance, godliness; and to godliness, mutual affection; and to mutual affection, love. For if you possess these qualities in increasing measure, they will keep you from being ineffective and unproductive in your knowledge of our Lord Jesus Christ. But whoever does not have them is nearsighted and blind, forgetting that they have been cleansed from their past sins.

As Christians, we believe we have already been accepted and forgiven by God. Character development simply makes us effective and productive. As we grow in character, we actually bear more fruit in all that we do. Why then do we avoid character development and growth? A mature disciple of Jesus can identify areas of struggle without hiding or feeling shame.

What part of your character needs work? What are the things that keep tripping you up? What do others say about your faults and blind spots? Who is helping you work on your character flaws?

HEALING

Much of Jesus' ministry consisted of healing. In fact, when the religious leaders criticized Him, He reminded them that He had come for the sick who needed healing, not for those who were well. Clearly, Jesus was reminding them and us that we all need healing—physical, emotional, and spiritual.

As my last semester of my doctoral work was coming to a close, there was something weighing on my mind—I had no job. I had experienced so much early success in ministry that after adding another degree, I expected opportunities to abound. Nevertheless, there I was, married with three kids ages five, four, and two and no job. I cried out to God asking why He would prepare me in so many ways and then not open up a job for me.

At that point. I needed to find a job just to pay for a place to live and provide for my kids. I got a job as a fundraiser, a job I truly hated. It took every ounce of energy just to get up each day and head to work. I would pray in the car, or more accurately, yell at God for my position. After a few months, this is the conversation I had with God:

> GOD: Allen, I cannot use you yet for what I have prepared for you until you deal with the vast amount of judgment in your heart.
>
> ALLEN: Ok let's deal with it because I want to get back to what I was called to do. Wow a way forward! Can we just deal with that today?!
>
> GOD: It will take longer than a day.
>
> ALLEN: This week?
>
> GOD: Nope
>
> ALLEN: This month?
>
> GOD: Nope.
>
> ALLEN: How long?
>
> GOD: That is yet to be seen, but I will heal you if you let me.

Eighteen months later after times of confession, healing, repenting, and receiving the love of the Father, I was released to return to the work of my calling. He had needed to deal with my character first. He loved me too much to put me in situations that my character could not handle. He healed me of things that would hinder my effectiveness and witness.

When Peter denied Jesus three times on the eve of the crucifixion, we can imagine the shame and guilt he felt. When the resurrected Jesus met Peter the first time, what did He do? He had Peter proclaim his love for Jesus three times. You can imagine the healing effect this had on Peter's psyche. Subsequently, every time Peter thought of the threefold denial, he also remembered the threefold affirmation of his love for Jesus.

We all have been mistreated, abandoned, betrayed, hurt, wounded, and disappointed; and, those things affect our character. But, I have come to understand that a mature disciple of Christ can tell you what character deficiency they are working on, a deficiency that comes from their core wounding, the healing they are currently seeking, and who is helping them in the process.

He longs to heal our wounds, emotions, losses and trauma. What are your rhythms of healing? What are the places that you do not fully trust God with? What are the core woundings that affect your life and relationships? What are you asking Jesus to heal you of?

UNDERSTANDING YOUR GIFTS

> Now about the gifts of the Spirit, brothers and sisters, I do not want you to be uninformed (1 Corinthians 12:1).

Watching Michael Jordan or Tiger Woods in their prime was inspiring. They displayed a talent that transcended their respective sport. Watching someone who has a gift that has been developed to the best of their ability is, I believe, a testament to God. Whether these athletes recognized where their gifts came from is debatable, but the stewardship of their gift is glorifying to God.

We all are wired to know our gifts and use and steward them to the best of our ability to the glory of God—not for fame or riches. We all want to live a life full of purpose and satisfaction that bears much fruit.

As Christians we first get clarity about our calling and then, secondly, clarity about our gifting. It is important to be informed about our natural gifts, spiritual gifts, learned gifts, personality, emotional wiring, and our role in the Body of Christ.

I love music and love to sing; however, I have no musical gifting. During seminary, I was told that I was expected to sing the liturgy during a service at the school. I told the professor that I had no ability to sing and that my singing would make a mockery of the service. Nevertheless, she told me that she could work with me and get me to a place of competence. After three days and many hours, she turned to me and apologized. She said, "You are right; you have no ability to pull this off!"

I have always wondered why we think we should have all the gifts. Why do we expect others to have all the gifts? And, more importantly, why do we continue to plod along in areas of incompetence when clearly another member of the body of Christ should be doing that work?

Some gifts were given to us at birth—athletic, intellectual, musical, linguistic . . . Other gifts we learn like public speaking, being a good spouse, writing or composing. Then there are the spiritual gifts for the building up of the body of Christ.

What are your natural gifts, learned gifts, and spiritual gifts? How do you go about getting clarity on your gifting? What do others confirm are your gifts? How are you working on your gifting? Do you find yourself spending lots of time and energy outside of your gifting?

(Again, I remind you for more discussion on these rhythms and habits, listen to the podcast at TheGoodsoil.us)

YELLOW FLAGS OF EQUIPPING

Now that we have discussed the healthy habits that lead to good soil. It is helpful to identify the pests and poisons that will harm the soil. What are the warning signs to look for when we are being equipped? How do we get off track? What are the temptations that keep us away from being properly equipped?

Acting Before Equipping

When my youngest son was four years old, he came out of the bathroom pouting and trying to hide his chin, which was bleeding profusely. I rushed over and started to clean his wound. It was clearly a straight cut, right across his chin. He was reluctant to tell me what had happened, but after some cajoling, he confessed that he had been shaving. Earlier that day he had seen me teaching his older brother to shave, and he wanted to be a big boy like that. I told him it was dangerous, and that when he grew up, I would teach him how to handle a razor safely. Just like my son, many of us get way ahead of ourselves. We dive into action before our time, before we have been trained and equipped and have matured.

While the incident with my son was cute, it could have left a scar. How many of us have jumped into action prematurely without proper training or maturing and have left scars on ourselves and others? I am afraid this has become the rule rather than the exception in Christian ministry.

I wonder if we think Jesus was an ineffective leader because He did not really do much before the age of thirty. He chose the hard work of being equipped before He was released into His public ministry. What was He doing from age eighteen to thirty? Nothing important? Or was He maturing in faith, developing His character and training?

When Christians get a sense of calling, with some inkling of their gifting, they get excited and far too often move straight to action. We should be excited, and we certainly want to be faithful to our call. However, we should take time to understand and develop our gifts before we leap into using them.

When called to do something, healthy disciples learn to ask the Lord and the church to equip them for the work, to help them identify and hone their gifts, and to surround them with others with similar calls. Jesus warns us not to go out on our own to minister in His Name unless we have been sent:

> Not everyone who says to me, 'Lord, Lord,' will enter the kingdom of heaven, but only the one who does the will of my Father who is in heaven. Many will say to me on that day, 'Lord, Lord, did we not prophesy in your name and in your name drive out demons and in your name perform many miracles?' Then I will tell them plainly, 'I never knew you. Away from me, you evildoers!' (Matthew 7:21–23)

The Christian life does not mean using our gifts and getting results. The Christian life means only using our gifts to do the things He calls us to do.

How many times have you gotten ahead of God? What are you doing to ensure you are using your gifts in alignment with your calling? How have those around you complimented your gifts? What gift do you have that you are trying to improve?

Never Equipped Enough

I can remember teaching an adult education class at my church. The room was full of people who wanted to learn and grow. Pouring myself into the class, I prepared well, researched great examples, and taught my heart out.

After the class, the participants said they really enjoyed the class. Many then asked, "When is the next class?" Then it hit me! Most of these people had been going from class to class for decades. I wondered why they were not trying to go out and live what was being taught.

I approached some of them to suggest that they take the principles of the class and try putting them into action. This is where I lost most of them. Many of them responded that they were not ready and that they needed to learn more. Somehow in my church, we had fostered a culture for Christians who wanted to learn more and more but were never ready to act on what they had learned. It seemed the undercurrent of thought was: "We do not have all the answers, so we are not willing to risk stepping out. You are the professional, we know because we pay you. You go out and do the work. We will keep enjoying the process of learning."

There and then, I decided never to teach or train unless there was an expectation that the training or teaching would be put into practice. You could see the shock on the faces of people whom I would not let into my next class because they had failed to do anything after the previous class.

In the last section, I said not to go out until you had been trained. Now you may wonder if I am reversing that and saying you should go out and do ministry before being fully trained? I get it. It is a balance. We are never fully trained. Some go out too soon while others wait too long. Which one are you?

Jesus sent His disciples out before they were fully trained. They were trained but not fully matured. He knew what He was doing. He knew that the next training could only happen after they had tried and failed. When His disciples returned from their ministry opportunity, they had questions they never would have had until they tried.

Jesus kept repeating the cycle of training, sending, more training, and sending again. It is actually impossible to be fully equipped before you act. This is why we will always need seasons of equipping.

Surgeons do not go straight from the classroom to the operating table. They train and practice the learned skills under other surgeons. Then they do surgery under supervision until they are released to operate without supervision.

Since eternal life is certainly more important than any surgery, I wonder why we do not have better systems of training. What are your rhythms of training? Are you scared to act on your training because you know you are not fully equipped? Who is helping you understand when it is time to go out and when is it time to train?

Inability to Identify Weaknesses

In the show "The Office," the main character Michael Scott was in a job interview and was asked to state his greatest weakness. His response was "I work too hard, I care too much, and sometimes I can be too invested in my job."

Too many of us have similar responses. We are not in touch with our weaknesses, our blind spots, and our habitual behaviors that cause harm to others. We believe weakness makes us vulnerable or is something to be ashamed of or that identifying our weakness will harm us.

I have a saying: "People will either make fun of you to your face or behind your back. You want it to your face." The reality is that we all have weaknesses, and no matter how hard we try, we cannot hide them from others. If we are mature disciples, we will create a culture where others feel comfortable talking about or joking about our weaknesses in front of us.

If they do it behind your back, it is because they think you are unaware or unreceptive or unwilling to address your weaknesses. We are reluctant to give people feedback when we think they are not mature enough to handle the truth.

I have worked with a lot of pastors, and this statistic amazes me—95% of them say they are above average preachers. How can this be? Logic tells us only 50% can be above average. They all report that their parishioners often tell them how good they are at preaching. I wonder how many of their congregants would feel comfortable telling them they were below average.

What are your weaknesses? Can you articulate them to others? Do others feel comfortable talking about your weakness in front of you? Do you get defensive, or are you able to own your limitations?

Not Comfortable in Your Own Skin

When my sons were young, they would tell me they wanted to be cowboys. They would dress up in the hat with the holster and the chaps. Then the next week they wanted to be firemen. Again, they would don the hat and uniform pretending to put out fires and rescue people. The next week, they wanted to be Spiderman and so on. That is normal behavior for a child.

They are trying to figure out who they are and where they fit. They are wondering what they would be good at, what they are gifted to do, and what would be fun.

But we have all met that person with no sense of who they are. They bounce around from one thing to the next. They are always trying to be something they are not. When they tell us what the next plan is, we simply shrug. We describe these people as not being comfortable in their own skin. What was cute for kids is tragic for us as adults.

Generally, these are people who have not had the where-with-all to stick to the thing they are called to do and do the hard work of training and maturing. They find they are not immediately good at something, so they move on to the next thing. They lack perseverance. They avoid growth.

If one is doing this with their job, it is sad, but when they are doing this as a husband or father it is tragic. If we are called to marriage or parenthood, it will require training. We will have to persevere.

Are you comfortable with who you are? With what you have accomplished? With how others see you? With what God has called you to be and do? Do you persevere in the areas He has appointed for you?

Identity Tied to Wrong Things

I like Sammy. I really do, but he has a habit that drives me crazy. Inevitably, when we are talking, he will name drop. He has just met with this important person, or he is friends with this famous person, or he got a call from so and so who is the expert on the topic we are discussing. Any chance he gets, he posts pictures of himself with some famous Christian.

Similarly, we have all encountered the guy who is constantly telling you what they have accomplished; how many people showed up to their last whatever; how much money they make; how popular and cool they are; and how many degrees and letters they have after their name, ad infinitum. They are always giving you their resume.

Over-emphasis on status, position, title, wealth, or name is an indication of insecurity or an identity issue. As Christians, our identity should be secure in Christ. At the heart of identity issues, is the need for character development and maturity. We believe false narratives about who we are and make up new ones to define ourselves in a way we hope will draw others.

We all want to be known. But, when we use false identities to attract people to us, we still end up alone. We fear being found out. Mature

Christians do the hard work of establishing their identity as sons and daughters of God. This takes equipping and maturing.

Where do you get your identity? Who authentically knows you? For what are you known—your accomplishments or your character?

Not Involved in Learning

To hear of anyone following a vocation that does not involve continuing education always concerns me. I would hope that everyone has the humility to know they do not know everything about their job.

Last week, I was hanging out with my brother, a neurologist, and he had received a book in the mail. Hoping it was a good book he would share with me, I asked what he was reading. To my disappointment, it was a preparation book for the test he had to take so that he could remain a neurologist. He explained to me that doctors have to take tests regularly to remain licensed. They need to keep up with the latest drugs, procedures, practices, and developments. Their training never ends.

Likewise, being a disciple means being a lifelong learner. Good doctors like my brother enjoy this process. He likes to read up on the latest advances in his field. He cares for his patients and is committed to giving them the best care possible. He knows that to do so, he must continue to learn. As Christians, we too are committing to continuing discipleship education.

Ever since childhood, I have loved keeping aquariums—another ongoing learning process. I listen to podcasts, watch YouTube videos, and talk with other hobbyists. I love learning more because it enables me to better care for the life in my tanks.

Christians likewise should desire to learn more about their faith. There is no end to growing in the Christian faith. We should be excited about learning to be a Christian mother or a student of good theology or a nurse who cares for the sick or a neighbor who shares their faith in this changing culture or an artist creating works that draw people to God through beauty.

There should be a yellow flag in your heart when you have no desire to learn. What are you reading? Who are you learning from? What training event are you attending? What are you excited to learn next about your faith?

No Order

As a twenty-year-old, my approach to discipleship was completely ad hoc. I studied or read the things that interested me most and chose to attend conferences that covered areas of discipleship I wanted to ponder. I had a very consumerist understanding of what discipleship looked like.

My training lacked any sense of order. There were no outside voices that encouraged me to train in areas that I was avoiding or were unknown to me. As the captain of the ship sailing wherever and whenever I wanted, I often got way ahead of God and myself. I wanted to learn the finer points before I had learned the basics.

Imagine joining the army and saying, "Hey, I will pass on basic training. I want to lead a tank division" or "I do not need training in artillery" or "I just want to start as a commander and learn commander things." That's not the right order.

Unfortunately, the church has fallen prey to the consumerist path, and all too often, there is no helpful sequencing of discipleship. Instead, we offer a buffet table where people pick and choose. In our Christian communities, we need to seek a place where those more mature than we are will walk with us down a path of discipleship, a path that lays a foundation, a path that builds on that foundation, and a path that covers all the aspects of discipleship. There is an art in creating, sequencing, and pacing someone through Christian formation.

Are you willing to relinquish the role of sole decision-maker in your Spiritual formation? What are your consumeristic tendencies in discipleship? Where can you find a healthy discipleship path with mature Christians to help you with healthy rhythms and sequencing?

Tyranny of the Urgent

We live in a world that has tireless competitors for our time, attention, and resources. There are multiple options of things to do every day of every week for everyone in my family. Many a Christian tells me, "Honestly, I'm just trying to keep my life working, trying to keep my head above water with all my responsibilities—job, marriage, bills, debt, kids. It takes all my energy to make it work. Where would I find time to be trained and equipped to be a disciple? So many things fill my schedule that I do not have time for discipleship."

Technology promises us more leisure but delivers a never-ending drain on our time, energy, and money. We are in a battle for our time. For success, we will fight on two fronts. One is innovatively figuring out ways to do discipleship in our current life and schedule. We need to figure out ways to transform our drive to work, our lunch breaks, and our morning family rituals. We also will need to figure out ways to stand firmly against the culture and say "No" to things so that we can say "Yes" to discipleship.

Where does discipleship fit into your schedule? How much time a week do you devote to discipleship? What do you give up for discipleship? What can you transform into times of discipleship? What competes most for your time and attention?

Want to explore your Equipping? We invite you to go to TheGoodSoil. us for more on Equipping.

8

The Good Soil of Community

ONGOING CYCLE OF DISCIPLESHIP

ONCE YOU ARE CALLED and equipped, you will walk out your ministry within the body of Christ. Christian community is not an option or an "add on" but is the context in which you live out your calling in faithfulness. The body of Christ is there to help, encourage, challenge, love, correct, teach, and bless you and speak the truth in love to you. (See 1 Corinthians 12–13.)

I grew up in a great neighborhood. My mother, father, two brothers, and I spent countless hours together. We played sports in the yard, fished in the pond down the road, and played cards, chess and Monopoly. My grandparents lived in the neighborhood. They were always home and welcomed us over for cookies and sodas that were not available at home. My first cousins, aunts, uncles and many other relatives also lived in the neighborhood. Family surrounded me. I was known; people were looking out for me. They were also keeping me in check which meant that I could not get away with anything!

I had many friends. Often a group of ten to fifteen played Kick the Can or Capture the Flag. We knew each other's parents and each other's dogs. We played on the same baseball teams and went to the same camps. There were always things to do and people to do it with. I felt safe in my neighborhood and fondly remember the community and the many shared holiday celebrations. This community was formative for me, and that seemed like the norm to me.

No, it was not perfect, and eventually much of it unraveled. My parents got divorced, friends moved away, and new rules required fencing in our dogs. But, there was something at the core of that community that spoke to me as a child and that I still yearn for today. As a Christian, I know we are to be a community that loves each other well, that plays and prays together, that is a place where we are fully known and loved, and a place that looks out for us and keeps us in check. I know internally that I was made for community and long for that community to be meaningful.

JESUS MODELS COMMUNITY

Jesus created a community that is the perfect model for discipleship. During His three-year earthly ministry, He primarily focused on forming a committed community that would, after His death, be the core of the Christian church. This tightly knitted community was comprised of a small group of men and women who followed Him throughout His ministry and gathered together after His death and resurrection.

Jesus' message: "If you want to be discipled, I invite you to be a part of a tight-knit community around which life is ordered. In this community, you will learn, grow, ask questions, and have opportunities to live out your faith and practice your gifts. You will watch me, eat with me, talk with me, and I will disciple you to be who God created you to be.

JESUS TEACHES COMMUNITY

Throughout His teaching ministry, Jesus focused on principles to live by. He taught Christians to strengthen and solidify their relationships with God and with one another. In fact, there are fifty-nine "one another" verses in the New Testament. Jesus used them, and His disciples repeated them in the epistles. Jesus taught that being one of His disciples meant being in community with one another.

In the Sermon on the Mount, Jesus teaches at length about the way one's heart should be inclined towards loving one's neighbor and enemies. As He teaches, He creates images of people living side by side in love and forgiveness:

> Therefore, if you are offering your gift at the altar and there remember that your brother or sister has something against you, leave your gift there in front of the altar. First go and be reconciled to them; then come and offer your gift. (Matthew 5:23–24)

For Jesus, relationships of love and forgiveness are far more important than religious acts. He tells us that loving one's neighbor is at the heart of all of God's teachings. (See Matthew 22:39–40.) Living in and participating in healthy community, not a group of individuals merely following rules, is the soil that grows fruitful disciples.

JESUS PRAYS FOR COMMUNITY

As Jesus prepares to leave this world, He underlines the principle of community as the way of life. He offers up a prayer to His Father in heaven. He prays for His disciples "that they may be one as we are one" (John 17:11). Furthermore, His prayer continues to include the grafting of future believers into community:

> My prayer is not for them alone. I pray also for those who will believe in me through their message, that all of them may be one . . . that they may they be brought to complete unity. Then the world will know . . . (John 17:20–21, 23b)

The purpose of this community is not just for the common life of believers but for the ongoing advancement of God's Kingdom on earth, serving as a witness to those who do not know the Lord and drawing them to Him.

JESUS EXPANDS COMMUNITY

Throughout His life, Jesus spent time with those on the outskirts of community—the leper, the widow, the adulterer, and the tax collector. Jesus always invited those on the outside inside. He drew others into community and instructed His disciples to do the same. Jesus had a clear message for us to take care of the "least of these," and by doing so, Christians would be taking care of Him. (See Matthew 25:31–46.)

Jesus was not simply instructing us to serve the least of these. Rather, since all are created in His image, we should serve them and draw them into the community. Even as Jesus was dying on the cross, He welcomed the criminal who was being crucified next to Him into His Kingdom, into the community of all of the saints gathered in eternity with the Lord. (See Luke 23:43.)

PAUL AND COMMUNITY

In his epistles to the church at Corinth and the church at Rome, Paul warned against division:

> I appeal to you, brothers, in the name of our Lord Jesus Christ, that all of you agree with one another so that there may be no divisions among you and that you may be perfectly united in mind and thought. (1 Corinthians 1:10 NIV 1984)

He further developed this idea of community by introducing the analogy of the church as a body, the body of Christ. He said, "So in Christ we, who are many form one body, and each member belongs to all the others" (Romans 12:5 NIV 1984). The church is not "many bodies" but "one body" with many parts. Again he wrote, "The body is a unit, though it is made up of many parts; and though all its parts are many, they form one body. So it is with Christ" (1 Corinthians 12:12 NIV 1984). Using the image of bread, Paul says that "because there is one loaf, we, who are many, are one body, for we all partake of the one loaf" (1 Corinthians 10:17 NIV 1984).

Paul is unambiguous about the fact that the actions of any member affect the other members, whether they intend them to do so or not. Furthermore, Paul explains that the job of each member of the body is to minister to the other members of the body. This ministry will attract others into the one body.

The power of being one with Jesus and one with one another may be difficult to imagine as a reality; however, when this happens there is an extraordinary phenomenon that takes place. When Christians live as one in body, then they will accomplish all that God has called them to do. Furthermore, they will even be able to do greater things than Jesus. (See John 14:12.)

Paul says the way to be fruitful in Christ is through the work of the body: "So, my brothers, you also died to the law through the body of Christ, that you might belong to another, to him who was raised from the dead, in order that we might bear fruit to God" (Romans 7:4 NIV 1984).

As Christians learn that they actually belong to one another, they live into the power of the resurrection, and they will bear the fruit of effective ministry. This concept is at the heart of Paul's teaching on discipleship.

Paul uses twenty "one another" statements that undergird his entire message. Christians are "to love one another" (Romans 13:8). Christians are to "excuse" one another (Romans 2:15 ESV). They are to "serve one another" (Galatians. 5:13). They are to forgive one another. (See Ephesians 4:32.) They are to "teach and admonish one another" (Colossians 3:16). Paul's message is clear that this commitment to living as one body is not an option but is the way of all who follow Christ: "Now you are the body of Christ, and each one of you is a part of it" (1 Corinthians 12:27).

In his famous discourse on love in 1 Corinthians 13, Paul illustrates the love that should characterize Christian brothers and sisters. This description of love portrays a community that all mankind would surely join if they had the opportunity.

PETER'S DESCRIPTION OF COMMUNITY

As Peter instructs the church, he creates an image of community grounded in the Old Testament and founded by Jesus as He modeled the power of community life:

> As you come to him, the living Stone—rejected by humans but chosen by God and precious to him—you also, like living stones,

are being built into a spiritual house to be a holy priesthood, offering spiritual sacrifices acceptable to God through Jesus Christ.
(1 Peter 2:4–5)

Peter paints an image that Christians are stones laid so closely to one
another that they form a single unit. Likewise, as Christians in the church,
they are to relate so closely with one another that they act as one and see
as one.

Also tied into this image is the relationship Christians have to Christ.
He is the cornerstone with which every rock aligns. As Christians align
with Him, it is inevitable that they will line up with one another. He is the
foundation upon which Christians build relationships with one another.

Without Christ as the cornerstone, the house would surely fall. And
on the cornerstone we align more stones that form the walls of the house.
These stones can be straight because they rest on the cornerstone. These
stones represent the people. They are laid very close to one another to create
appropriate walls and a secure home. These close relationships with each
other form the house. Building these walls is foundational for the church.
The house contains both Christ's' relationship to us and our relationship to
one another.

This building of walls directs the way the Church relates to the world.
Christians build the house to attract others to come inside. The community
of believers represents the walls within which the world can find salvation
and hope. If Christians do not build the house on the rock of Christ and
on the walls of commitment to a loving community, they fail to live into a
biblical view of the Church of Jesus Christ.

OTHER NEW TESTAMENT TEACHINGS ON COMMUNITY

Christians are admonished by the author of Hebrews against abandoning
the call to community: "Let us not give up meeting together, as some are in
the habit of doing, but let us encourage one another—and all the more as
you see the Day approaching" (Hebrews 10:25 NIV 1984).

This warning follows an explanation that as Christians they are
cleansed from unrighteousness, washed in "pure water," and instructed to
persevere in the faith. They are told to "hold unswervingly to the hope we
profess" and to "consider how we may spur one another towards love and
good deeds" (Hebrews 10:23, 24).

Christians encourage each other to be immersed in the life of community, for it is the way of love. Community is the source from which encouragement flows like living water. Christians must not be tempted to live without community.

In the book of Acts, the power and centrality of community codifies the Church. When Jesus sent the Church the Holy Spirit to guide and comfort them, He chose a time when they were gathered as a community. The Holy Spirit came at Pentecost when "they were all together in one place" (Acts 2:1).

After the coming of the Holy Spirit upon the disciples and the fruit that followed, Christians continued to gather in community: "Every day they continued to meet together in the temple courts. They broke bread in their homes and ate together with glad and sincere hearts" (Acts 2:46). They recognized the power of connection with one another in the Holy Spirit.

Certainly, the disciples were thinking of Jesus' words, "For where two or three come together in my name, there am I with them" (Matthew 18:20). This coming together was what scripture calls *ekklesia* or church. Christians must remember "church" was not a building to the early Christians. Church was the people of God, filled with the Spirit, and gathered as a body.

THE TRINITY IS COMMUNITY

In Genesis 1, God is referred to multiple times as "us." We see that both His Word and His Spirit have a role in creation. And when God discusses the concept of creating man, He says, "Let us make mankind in our image, to be like us" (26 ISV). God is an "us" and when we are created in His image, we by definition are in need of another. The one thing that was NOT good before the fall was man being alone.

Kallistos Ware describes the Trinitarian God this way:

> The Christian God is not just a unit but a union, not just a unity but community. There is in God something analogous to 'society.' He is not a single person, loving Himself alone, not a self contained monad or 'The One.' He is trinity: Three equal persons, each one dwelling in the other two by virtue of an unceasing movement of mutual love. Amo ergo sum, 'I love, therefore I am.'[1]

---

1. Kallistos Ware, *The Orthodox Way* (New York: St. Vladimir's Press, 1986), 33.

The Trinity is not primarily a theological doctrine to be analyzed as much as it is an icon of love to be emulated. When discipleship is reduced to understanding or the study of God, the whole body suffers. Hope in the Gospel is not in understanding but rather in participation in community, where Christians share and partake in the love of God.

The notion of a triune God who lives in community at all times is such a radical idea. When Jesus insists that God is Father and that He and the Father are one, He makes a claim that expands our understanding of the divine and of our relationship to God. His claim was so radical that the religious leaders wanted to kill Him for His declaration.

God is community, and we are invited into this community where we can have life and life abundant, or we can choose isolation and the inevitable death that follows that choice. So, stay with me because in the next chapter we will look at the key components of Christian community.

9

Working the Soil of Community

DISCIPLESHIP IS INTENDED TO be life on life. It is not primarily to be self-discovered but rather handed down, shared, given away and modeled effectively. Discipleship presumes a heart connection between the parties. Jesus is the model. He did it in and through the incarnation. His success was an established community not a huge number of disciples. The fruit was born out of the time they spent with one another.

Like many Americans, I love watching football. The excitement of a big play, a great catch, or last second touchdown is downright contagious. But there seems to be a trend in the NFL to celebrate and promote individuals rather than the team.

I joined a fantasy football league in which you pick players from different teams and your score is the summation of their achievements. Here is the crazy thing—now, when I watch I am not rooting for a team but for individuals. After one play I celebrated when my receiver caught a long pass, but on the next play I complained because his teammate, a running back who was on my brother's fantasy team scored a touchdown. My eight-year-old son said, "Dad, I don't understand. Which team are you cheering for?"

Football is supposed to be a team game. In reality, it is a team game. Despite any one person's individual effort or talent, every play is dependent on others. Someone has to hike, and someone has to handoff or pass the ball. Others are blocking or taking defenders away from the action. Someone is calling the play. Someone else devised the play that was called. Any given play never involves only one person.

Likewise, Christianity is a team sport. It is not for individuals. Too often we focus on and even celebrate individual Christians' success instead of the success of the community. Just like football fruitfulness is never the result of one individual's actions but is always a result of community effort. When a popular evangelist preaches and many commit their lives to Christ, he should know that he is simply reaping where others have plowed and sowed.

With this in mind, let's look at some key concepts of community that I believe will help us leave behind the individualism of our culture so we can better experience the fullness of true community.

HEALTHY RHYTHMS AND HABITS OF COMMUNITY

The Incarnational Nature of Discipleship

We all love compliments. We love it when others point out something that we have done or accomplished. Of all the compliments I have received, the most meaningful is when I have been told, "Man, I really like just being with you."

Other compliments tend to point out a gift well used or some successful outcome. Conversely, the above compliment is, at its core, a statement that someone knows and enjoys me and wants to be in community with me. Discipleship is more than highlighting the successes of life, rather it is doing life joyfully with others.

Christianity stands alone in its teaching that God desires our community even though we are flawed. The decision of an all-powerful, all knowing God to lower Himself to become man is astounding. Why would a perfect God really want to hang out with me with all of my flaws, limitations, and outright rebellion against Him? We forget the plan all along was for God to delight in being and spending time with us.

When we remove the incarnational nature of discipleship, it becomes mere religion which is not what God desires. Remember that Jesus criticized the Pharisees at length for their religious spirit. He clearly exposed them for burdening people with teachings and rules. In their pursuit of doing right, they had lost the incarnational nature of discipleship.

They had put aside and devalued the simple importance of walking and talking and being with the people. They became more interested in walking with the right people, the clean people—at least on the outside.

They were not willing to walk with those whom they deemed unworthy or to get involved in lives that were too messy.

Jesus tells a parable to get their attention on this matter. He tells them of a man who was beaten and left on the side of the road. In this story the religious leaders passed by the hurt and wounded man. They avoided him because he was unclean. If the priest touched blood of an unclean man, he would have to wait to do his priestly duties. If people saw the religious leaders helping an unclean person, his reputation might have been at risk. In short, it would have been a real hassle for a religious person to help this injured man.

Then a nobody, some unclean person, a Samaritan, came by and helped the man, bound his wounds, took care of him and paid for his lodging until he was well. Jesus asked the Pharisees which one had acted in accordance with the will of God? Obviously, it was the man who met the true needs of the robbed and injured man. Jesus instructed them and us to go and do likewise. He was saying that true discipleship is dealing with the hassles and the messy nature of humanity while showing love regardless of the cost.

We need to recover the understanding that discipleship means life together. Discipleship means eating meals, celebrating birthdays, and crying together over loss and tragedy. Discipleship means sharing experiences that reveal one another's hearts.

What makes incarnational discipleship harder is that when we lovingly share our lives with others, they do not always reciprocate. Often they reject us. Remember: Jesus poured His life into a small number of disciples. They rejected Him, denied Him, and abandoned Him, and Judas turned him over to death.

True discipleship forces us to a level of vulnerability that happens only when life is shared. In the age of social media, we can easily convince ourselves that we are doing life with others through technology. Unfortunately, while people have thousands of friends on Facebook, we as a people have never felt so lonely and isolated. We choose to live vicariously through select images and a feigned reality. Yet we cannot squelch our deep desire to be fully known.

Community and Time Commitment

When Jesus invites the twelve to join Him as His disciples, we do not get much of the story. In essence, He says, "Drop everything you are doing and follow Me." I can imagine there was some discussion even if only among themselves or with friends and family. It might have gone like this: "Peter, how long are you going? When will you be back? What kind of commitment is Jesus asking of you? Can I have your fishing nets?"

What I think was clear is that it was going to be for a time. People in that day understood the time commitment of becoming the disciple of another. They knew it was not a weekend retreat. It was going to take a season or two. This was not going to be a weekend retreat.

Now we live in a culture that continuously puts more and more demands on our time and attention. One of the biggest challenges we all face is the question of where to give our time and energy? The church reports having a hard time competing with the culture. Some churches believe they must try to pack all discipleship into a Sunday morning corporate worship service because it is the only time, we have the people's attention.

But what we are learning is that a Sunday morning corporate service simply cannot deliver the fullness of discipleship no matter how excellent it is. A great sermon, great music, and large gathering of people does not translate into people being deeply transformed and ready to face the troubles and challenges of our world and culture.

Discipleship cannot be done on our terms and in a set amount of time. It takes commitment in a world where commitments are often not honored. Jesus is inviting us to sacrifice time, expense, and convenience to be His disciples. Our calendar is a good window into our commitments.

Where in your schedule do you plan to be discipled? What are you intentional about? What does your calendar reveal about your priorities?

Hard Conversations in Community

A friend of mine invited me to lunch. I was expecting him to ask me for some advice or help. Instead, he confronted me on my attitude on the soccer field. He pointed out that as a Christian and a pastor perhaps I should not act like a jerk while playing soccer. This was a hard conversation to have.

When my friend tells the story, he explains that he thought he was taking a big risk. He thought maybe by calling me out on my behavior, he might lose a friend. Instead, what happened was a good conversation that led me to confession and repentance. I knew I was behaving badly. I was a bit embarrassed but was thankful that he was willing to bring it into the light. Our friendship grew deeper that day because we trusted one another more. Since then, he has become one of my best friends, and we often do ministry together.

Discipleship involves the willingness and ability to have hard conversations. If hard conversations are so fruitful, why do so many of us avoid them?

Many people equate hard conversations with conflict. In their experience with hard conversations, someone has tried to defend themselves resulting in the conversation getting out of hand. Words are spoken out of pain and anger, and feelings are hurt. Enter the fear of losing a relationship. Certainly, hard conversations sometimes lead to conflict. But, when done in love, they are often welcomed without conflict.

Others have experienced someone having a hard conversation with them not presented in a loving manner. They felt judged, condemned, and belittled. So, the next time they see a hard conversation coming their way, they avoid it at all cost.

Do you avoid the hard conversations? Do you have hard conversations in a loving manner? Do you think all hard conversations will bring conflict?

Jesus gives us an example of a difficult conversation in an exchange with Peter. He is preparing for the greatest trial of His life; He is responding to the call of His Father to face death on the cross. He has prayed and gotten clarity, but man's will, or common sense, or just good-natured optimism attempts to derail Him. Jesus has affirmed Peter. His identity is set. Yet He still must confront Peter when this disciple out of his affection for Jesus, tries to talk Him out of obeying the Father and heading to the cross. Jesus rebukes Peter, "Get behind me Satan."

While Jesus' words may have seemed harsh, we know that Jesus responded to Peter out of love. He cared for Peter's soul. His desire was for Peter to learn to be sure when he spoke, that he did so from a place of having heard from the Lord and not from his own fleshly desires. Here, Peter was speaking out of his own desire for Jesus not to suffer; but this was not the Lord's will. So, out of love, Jesus rebukes him. Notice Peter is not undone. He does not quit. He does not defend himself. He does not think Jesus doesn't like him anymore. He receives Jesus' words.

A difficult conversation undergirded by prayer and coming from a place of humility and compassion for the other party is life giving. This is the key to both giving and receiving "a hard word." Most people appreciate honest conversation with someone who has compassion for them. This is how the Lord Himself deals with us. Remember His kindness leads us to repentance. (See Romans 2:4.)

With Paul, we see another example of the importance of the hard conversation at the Council of Jerusalem. Paul had to confront Peter on his treatment of Gentiles as second-class citizens. You can be sure people were saying in the parking lot, "Who does Paul think he is? Didn't he kill Christians? What right does he have to confront Peter?" But again, the exchange was done in love and bore fruit. They were able to come up with a plan to lovingly minister to Gentiles in a different way than to the Jews.

However, even when discipleship is done well, the hard conversations may drive some away for a time or perhaps forever. The rich young ruler walked away from Jesus after a hard conversation. He was not ready for the sacrifice required to follow Jesus. We do not know if perhaps later he weighed the cost and decided to follow Jesus. Another time, Jesus told His followers they would have to eat His flesh and drink His blood. Again, some of His disciples walked away because His sayings were too hard.

How often do you have hard conversations? When do you begin a hard conversation? Do you know how to have them in love? What is the outcome of your hard conversations? How do you respond when someone initiates a hard conversation with you? Are you defensive? Do you fear conflict? Do you fear losing people over conflict?

Trust Fuels Healthy Community

Last year I was asked to help a church in a leadership transition. The lay leaders told me they wanted to bring someone in to help grow the church which had been in decline for a decade. Very soon into a meeting with the elder board, there was a strong sense of animus. As the discussion went on, emotions and opinions seemed to build to a point of contention. Finally, I asked one of the elders whom they trusted to make this decision. She replied, "I do not trust one person sitting in this room."

We then were able to get to the heart of the problem—there was no trust in the community. They did not trust the pastor, the staff, or each other. No wonder they could not grow. No wonder they could not make any decisions.

They needed to understand that their first priority was to get to the root of all the distrust in the community and then go through a process of healing and repentance. Everything else was secondary. Trust is the currency of relationship. With no trust there can be no relationship.

Trust is the fuel that makes communities run. Trust is the fabric that holds communities together. 1 Corinthians tells us that love always trusts. The Christian community must be a place of high trust. Without trust discipleship can never happen.

We have all been in communities or families or on teams with low trust. This is difficult and taxing on the individuals. Stephen Covey in his book, *Speed of Trust*, explains that in a high-trust community, you can say the wrong thing, and people will still get your meaning. In a low-trust community, you can be very measured, even precise, and they'll still misinterpret you.

Who do you trust? Is your Christian community a trusting community? What breaks trust? How is trust restored?

Perseverance in Community

In a recent book called *Grit,* Angela Duckworth identified the quality that would best predict the success of a West Point cadet to endure the grueling training. It was not who had the highest IQ. It was not the best athletes. It was the ability to stay with the program no matter the cost. She calls this quality "grit."

Scripture calls it perseverance. Paul tells us the life of a disciple will include suffering and "suffering produces perseverance; perseverance, character; and character, hope" (Romans 5:3–4). Disciples persevere through suffering. This does not mean that we will avoid failure. We will blow it from time to time. The willingness to persevere means we are so sure in our relationship with God that our only response is to get back up and continue. This perseverance is the crucible that builds character.

Duckworth explains that this perseverance is a better predictor of success than intelligence, talent, athletic ability and other traits. The thing that demands perseverance is suffering, and suffering is the inevitable result of being with others. One's ability to deal with the inevitable suffering that comes with all relationships is the best predictor of who will be committed.

Every community will have people that cause suffering. This is true of your family, your friends, your neighbors, and your church. Christian community is not some utopia where everyone treats us well and loves us. Rather, we are a group of people who, in spite of meanness or treachery, continue in the ways of love; we persevere in love.

We get in trouble when we are always looking for better friends, better spouses, better families, and better churches instead of learning to persevere in the suffering that all community brings. Now certainly, the community of Christians must have character that rises above the communities of the world, or we will not attract others to our faith. Unfortunately, all too often, Christians desire community but show very little perseverance within community when things get hard and suffering occurs.

Suffering is core to understanding the cross. He suffered for our sins. He laid down His life for ours. As disciples we are being invited into that suffering, and as we persevere, we will experience hope that will shape us and draw others into the Christian faith.

Paul tells the Galatian church, "Let us not become weary in doing good, for at the proper time we will reap a harvest if we do not give up" (Galatians 6:9). He understands that the Christian life is challenging; so, he reassures them that if they persevere, they will bear much fruit. We need this encouragement today. Discipleship demands perseverance.

What do you persevere in? What communities cause you suffering and what is your response? How do we train to increase in our perseverance? How would you describe the perseverance of the saints that are in your church family?

METHODS OF COMMUNITY

Discipleship has many different forms and delivery systems. It is helpful to understand the basic settings where we grow, train, and disciple others. Getting a grasp of which mode you are in or are delivering is critical. This helps us with proper expectations and shows us the places we are missing.

In short, discipleship entails learning and teaching, then space to think through and discuss the principles. Following that, discipleship requires that we try out these principles and train and improve upon them. We need to deeply process each concept and talk through our successes, failures, and questions. Finally, there comes a time to master them and to give them away.

DISCIPLESHIP MATURING

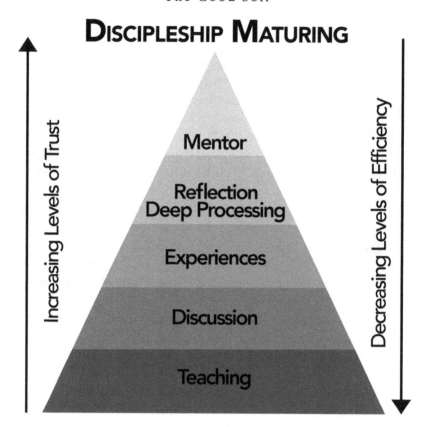

Increasing Levels of Trust

Decreasing Levels of Efficiency

Mentor

Reflection
Deep Processing

Experiences

Discussion

Teaching

Teaching

"Now when Jesus saw the crowds, he went up on a mountainside and sat down. His disciples came to him, and he began to teach them" (Matthew 5:1).

When I was in college, I loved to read C.S. Lewis and J.R.R. Tolkien. These books taught me much about the faith. Books like *Mere Christianity* spoke to my mind and helped me wrestle with the key concepts of the faith. Books like *The Chronicles of Narnia* and *The Lord of the Rings* taught me through imagination.

Jesus used parables because we need more than logical statements. We need to use both our left and right brains to fully understand a concept. Also, as humans we often cannot see our way until we see someone else's way first. Once we observe another, the concept moves beyond idea and becomes rooted. We then can better understand what this might look like for us.

Teaching is the first building block in discipleship. We desperately need to know the biblical and philosophical reasons behind the faith. We live in a world of competing agendas and thoughts. Reason and imagination are attacked on all sides. The Christian worldview gives us proper perspective on all things, and yet there are so many world views competing for our thoughts.

After Jesus called His disciples, He taught them the ways of the Kingdom of God and set them in contrast to the teachings of the world. With the Sermon on the Mount He used this same pattern: "You have heard it said . . . but I tell you . . ." (See Matthew 5:21–48.) Jesus knew His disciples needed to be taught how to distinguish the ways of God from all other teachings.

Teaching reaches the mind and gives us the necessary knowledge to live victoriously. Teaching helps us "not conform to the pattern of this world, but be transformed by the renewing" of our minds so that we "will be able to test and approve what God's will is—his good, pleasing and perfect will" (Romans 12:2). Teaching lays the foundation for discernment. Teaching prepares us to be able to "demolish arguments and every pretension that sets itself up against the knowledge of God" and "take captive every thought to make it obedient to Christ" (2 Corinthians 10:5).

Thankfully, in 21st century America, great teaching is fairly ubiquitous. We can listen to the great teachers and preachers of our day with the click of a button. We have instant access to all the greats before us on our phone or computer within seconds; however, we must be mindful that we are also more frequently assaulted with competing thoughts, teachings, and ideas.

As disciples, we will have hundreds of teachers in our lifetime. We will have teachers we have never met in books that we read. We will have teachers from different eras and different cultures. We will continue to learn and will continue to seek good teaching for the rest of our lives. We will always have more to learn and will always need to be reminded of what we have already learned and are not putting into practice. Teaching has lifelong value in the life of a disciple.

Initial Discussion

> Then he left the crowd and went into the house. His disciples came
> to him and said, 'Explain to us the parable of the weeds in the field.'
> (Matthew 13:36)

My favorite classes were never the ones consisting solely of lecture. My favorites were the ones where I could ask questions and process my thoughts on what was being taught. Some of my classes, though, were simply too big for space to be allowed to take the conversation in the direction I desired. Consequently, I had to find other places to satisfy that need.

The disciples had similar experiences. As Jesus was teaching the crowds, the disciples also heard the teaching, but they instinctively knew that they needed to wait until the crowd was gone to process the teaching with Jesus. They wanted to understand how to apply the teaching in their own lives.

There have been many studies on how adults learn best and how information actually gets translated into action and changed behavior. The result of these studies tells us we learn when we can do these things:

1. Hear and understand an idea.

2. Have time to process what the idea means to us.

3. Hear stories or see examples of how others have lived out the idea.

4. Discuss with others what it would look like to live out that idea in our own lives.

Simply sitting and listening to a teaching is just the beginning of learning and discipleship. Once we can mentally understand an idea, we need to process the idea. We need to ask questions. We need to think about what living out the idea would look like in this world and culture. What would that look like for me specifically to live out that idea? If I live out this idea what effect would it have on the rest of my life? Would I have to give up something? What would it cost me in terms of time and money? How will others see me differently if I did live this out? Do I know anyone who is living this out? What is the fruit of it?

Places of initial processing are critical for discipleship. Many of the tools/programs being developed in the church are adding this component. They are making sure there is time for people to get into small groups and discuss the teachings. They are creating workbooks, showing videos, and creating pictures of how others are applying the teaching. Then they are giving space for people to start the processing for their own lives.

Initial processing takes trust, time, intentionality and perseverance within the church community. Where do you get to process ideas? What groups are you part of that encourage you to think out loud and ask questions about the Christian life? What are the settings that most encourage you to process your thoughts and questions?

Experience

Now that we have been taught an idea and have discussed it, we are ready to go out and try to live out the concept. In my journey, I was taught what prayer was and had the opportunity to discuss what prayer could look like in my life. Then I had to go and pray. I had to experience what worked and what did not. I had to try things out to understand what I did and did not know.

Jesus taught his disciples, he discussed the ideas with them, and then he sent them out to do the work of ministry. They were not completely prepared. They did not have all the answers. But they needed to go out and experience the life so that they could grow deeper in their understanding. Jesus sends out the 12 and they return and discuss with him all that they did. We can assume they had both stories of success and failure. They had questions that they did not have before they went out. Jesus spent time with them discussing, processing, and teaching them more. Then he sent them out again and the process continued.

In James 1 we are told that after receiving the word we are to go do what it says. We are not just to keep on learning and learning without ever doing. Being a disciple means we will have to start putting our faith into practice. We will have to live into the ideas before we fully understand them.

Deep Processing

My first job in ministry was as a youth pastor. I had been a Christian for seven years, read lots of books, heard many sermons, been in small groups, and now I was being sent out to do ministry with teenagers.

I was petrified. I had no idea what to do. I was unsure of my preparedness, but I showed up and gave it my best. Some things went well; others fell flat. Then and only then was I ready to be discipled into deeper understanding of the faith. I did not know what I did not know until it was right in front of me.

I quickly found others who had gone before me and asked the questions I did not have until I was in the midst of doing the ministry. I was able to go deeper and grasp concepts that were previously foreign simply due to a lack of experience.

Jesus taught His disciples. He created space for them to come to Him and ask questions. He gave them instructions and sent them out to do ministry. They had successes and they had failures. They then returned to Jesus and entered into the next level of discipleship—deep processing. They learned to trust Jesus with all their hearts.

Initial processing of some concept of Christian discipleship will lead to a plan of action. We will go out and try to live our lives as disciples of Christ. We then will have more questions and experiences. We need to get some things right and be fruitful while other things will trip us up and leave us befuddled. Then we are ready to go even deeper in discipleship.

This step is very difficult for Christians to take. This requires a deep trust of the person(s) with whom we are processing. We are sharing our lives, our stories, and the heart of who we are. This is only possible with the people whom we trust enough to be transparent and open about everything. Deep processing happens when we feel safe enough to discuss our sins and failures. These are the deep friendships and mature marriages where we know and are known by others, where we are not judged but loved.

I lead retreats and lead them with a team of close friends. On these retreats, we have a lot of fun. We laugh, play, and eat together as we discuss struggles and share victories. In short, we do life together. We are a group that has been doing deep processing for a season. Inevitably, after each event we are asked by some if they can join our circle of friendship. They want to know how to get in.

We take this as a compliment because we know all of us are wired this way; and, it is a natural maturing that leads us to desire these relationships. In our evaluations, what becomes clear is that the participants' ability to see and be around a group that trusts and loves each other is rare and much sought after. We are often told that they have no friends and no one whom they trust enough to be transparent. They are frustrated because they have been exposed to teaching and light processing, and now, they want to go deeper.

This is all too common as many Christians report that they do not have these relationships and do not know how to get them. The church has struggled with the concept and ability to provide this for people for a few reasons. First, it is not very efficient to create this space because deep trust takes time and maturity. We cannot put a timeline on it. These trust-based relationships cannot be artificially manufactured and managed.

The church has created places of initial processing and uses the same tools and techniques in an effort to foster deep relationships. Many churches start small groups or community groups with the hope that the group will become a place where deep processing can happen. Sometimes they even use pressure to try to force the small group to meet that need.

To God's credit, sometimes this happens, and we praise God for that. But deep friendships are complicated and cannot be forced. What the church can do, however, is teach on deep friendships, allow people to understand and discuss (light processing), and then try to create fertile soil for these to develop naturally.

These relationships take work, they are hard, they do not always last forever, and you will be betrayed at some point. Nevertheless, the relationships are worth the pain, trouble, and sacrifice. We are created for these kinds of relationships, and without them we will suffer.

The primary place for all disciples to have this kind of deep relationship is with God. We need to come out of hiding and trust Him. We need to be able to share our hearts, our sorrows and disappointments with Him. Then we need to be able to move from deep intimacy with Him and have that type of intimacy with a select few with whom we can engage in deep processing.

Deep processing happens only after a disciple has been called, trained, equipped and sent. We often confuse deep processing with initial processing. Deep processing exposes our core wounding. One example is that it can shine a light on our rebellion against God and our neighbor. It is not a place for the defensive or fearful. Therefore, while it is to be desired, it is also often eschewed.

Deep processing is done in a group with a high level of trust. This requirement naturally limits the number of people within a group to two or three and rarely more than five. These groups are born out of relationship. Rarely are they something you can just sign up for. They are sought out and established through authentic vulnerability and a commitment to discipleship.

Do you have or desire a friend or spouse that fully knows you, your story, your best and your worst? Are you willing to go through the maturing process to be in a group like this? Do you need to address some emotional healing before you can trust others? What might be stopping you from these deep relationships?

Mentorship

The first time I met Terry, he had been hired as a consultant for our organization. I told my friend who was in charge, "I'll come for ten minutes, but then I might look down at my phone and ask to be excused for a prior engagement."

I had heard enough of these consultants to know they were all the same and not to be trusted. When Terry started to speak, however, I realized that he was speaking about the things that were most important in my heart. He was doing the things I dreamed of. He had the gifts I had and had refined them beyond my level.

Five hours later, I did not want the meeting to end. After that, Terry became a mentor to me. He recognized my potential and similar gifting and was willing to give of his time and talent to disciple me in many areas. Trust was built very quickly, hard conversations were the norm, and transformation in my life was the result.

Peter stands out among the twelve disciples. He gets a front row seat to some of the highlights with Jesus. He gets to go into the room with Jesus to raise Jairus's daughter from the dead. He is invited along with James and John to the Mount of Transfiguration. He walks on water for a while. For some reason, Jesus chose to mentor Peter in ways He did not with the other disciples.

I am sure other disciples wondered why he was chosen. This is a common human reaction. We all wonder why others seem to get into the inner circle and we are left out. C. S. Lewis in an article called "The Inner Ring" helps us understand two things about inner rings that certainly exist:

> First, they are inevitable because people with like minds and interests are drawn together. Unintentionally, this inner ring is formed around mutual desires, experiences, and interests. Secondly, it is tempting and dangerous to simply desire to be in an inner ring just because you have been left out. It tempts us to act like we are something we are not so that we can fit in or belong.[1]

1. C. S. Lewis. "The Inner Ring" (https://www.lewissociety.org/innerring).

Let me share with you why mentorships are so hard to find. The church cannot dictate or organize them although we try to anyway. Again, I know someone at this point will tell me a story of how the church set up a mentor program that worked great. I believe them and, yet I would say that this is an exception.

What I see work well is that the church exposes disciples to good teaching on mentorship, tells stories of good mentor experiences, encourages people to seek them out, and prays for that to happen. The job of the church is to promote and create healthy soil in which mentorships take root.

Among the common mistakes that have killed mentorships, is the failure to establish boundaries with clearly expressed requirements from either the mentor or mentee or both in terms of time and boundaries, and what is expected from each other. Good mentorships have good boundaries. All involved know the time frame, the content, the expected outcomes, and the agreed upon communication frequency. We all can learn to be good mentees and mentors.

I read a book about a guy who has a set program of mentoring. He has a specific time frame. He has an application process. He has a clear and specific agenda of the things he would cover. People applied, were approved, and it worked. Hallelujah!

So, he wrote a book and told everyone to do it just like he did. Oops! This is where things start to fail. People read the book and tried to do exactly what he did. They were not equipped to give away what he was giving to his mentors. They did not have the gifting to organize it the way he did. There were failures and frustrations.

We would love to make mentoring easy, efficient, predictable and orderly. We are all different both in the way we mentor and the way we receive mentoring from others. There is no perfect way to do it. It is messy, inefficient, and unpredictable. In spite of all that, it is well worth all the effort to pursue it.

If we are intentional and prayerful, we can hope to have five to ten mentors in our lifetime. These are people who have been down the road and are willing to be our guides for a season. Mentors last for a season and rarely last more than five years. Mentors certainly benefit from the relationship, but they sacrificially give of their time and experience to bless others in their walk.

If you have been mentored, expect that one day you will be charged to mentor others. If you want to mentor but have not had at least two mentors yourself, you are probably doing it too soon. Once someone is mentored, they are charged to go out and live the way they have been shown. We see this with Jesus and Peter. We also see it again repeated with Paul and Timothy. Listen to Paul describe his mentorship with young Timothy:

> You, however, know all about my teaching, my way of life, my purpose, faith, patience, love, endurance, persecutions, sufferings—what kinds of things happened to me in Antioch, Iconium and Lystra, the persecutions I endured. Yet the Lord rescued me from all of them. In fact, everyone who wants to live a godly life in Christ Jesus will be persecuted, while evildoers and impostors will go from bad to worse, deceiving and being deceived. But as for you, continue in what you have learned and have become convinced of, because you know those from whom you learned it. (2 Timothy 3:10–14)

Paul taught Timothy; he shared stories and experiences with him, the things he had learned. He took time to be with Timothy, to answer his questions and process his frustrations and failures. He mentored Timothy in the faith. He released him then to go out and continue in what he had learned and to mentor others in Christ.

Who have been your mentors? How did these relationships come about? How did they start? End? What have you been mentored in? What would you like to be mentored in next? What area might you be called to mentor others in? How can you be trained to be a good mentor?

FORMS OF DISCIPLESHIP IN COMMUNITY

As mentioned earlier discipleship is complex and involves all kinds of people in our lives. We will need teachers, counselors, coaches, mentors, advisors, friends, pastors, mentors, confessors, etc . . . Each of these is part of the discipleship process. Each is needed at certain times in our growth and maturing process. We will need different forms of discipleship in the ongoing process of discipleship. See the chart below I use to help people expand their understanding of discipleship. Which quadrant do you see yourself in now? Who is helping you? What is missing? Where do you serve others? What area do you thrive in when helping others?

YELLOW FLAGS OF COMMUNITY

Now that we see the importance of community and that community is the soil we live in, we turn our attention to the things that sabotage this soil, the things we need to be aware of as signs that we are not in a healthy community, the concepts that contend with the kind of community God wants from us.

Isolated, Lonely and/or Depressed

I don't think anyone really knows me.

I have a hard time getting motivated.

When I think about what my day holds for me it gets me down.

I have no excitement about my life or work.

15% of the US population has experienced depression, and the recent studies by Cigna Health Group on loneliness paint a picture of a pandemic where "most Americans consider themselves lonely."[2] In 2018 Great Britain appointed a minister for loneliness. This is a real problem. Community is under attack. Social media has tried to fill the gap, often unsuccessfully. People are losing the art of being in and committing to community, and the result is increased loneliness in epidemic numbers.

It is not good for man or woman to be alone. We are hardwired to be with others. Unfortunately, in a broken world, many of us have been so wounded or betrayed by others that we think it is a relief to be by ourselves.

We do not trust the communities we are part of enough to share deeply about who we are and who we are not. We settle for false community experiences hoping they will help us feel connected. Many are giving up hope that they could ever be deeply known and accepted by a community.

When Jesus died, the veil separating man from the Holy of Holies, the very presence of God, was torn in two. We now, through Jesus, have unfettered access to God. We have been invited into the community of the Trinity. As we live in this community as adopted sons and daughters, we can have true community with others. There is hope!

2. "New Cigna Study Reveals Loneliness at Epidemic Levels in America," May, 1,2018, https://www.cigna.com/newsroom/news-releases/2018/new-cigna-study-reveals-loneliness-at-epidemic-levels-in-america/

How lonely are you? How often do you feel alone even when you are in a crowd? What is your cure for loneliness? What community do you trust the most? What makes you feel connected with others?

Not Involved in Groups

I don't belong to any groups.

I keep to myself.

I don't fit in.

I'm not a joiner.

If you have no place to process or if you put all that pressure on one friend or your spouse, it will not hold. We need to be in the body of Christ to be a disciple. We have to push past the broken relationships, the lack of trust, and the wounding that keep us from being involved in groups where we are known.

The crucible that Jesus used to disciple the twelve was a small group. They ate together, talked together, fought with one another, dealt with jealousy, shared incredible experiences, witnessed miracles, suffered together, and celebrated together. By all account this was a ragtag group, but it was a place of deep community.

I can't help but think that many chose not to be His disciple or follow Him because they did not want to be in the community that He had formed. He had rough and tough fishermen. He had tax collectors. He had women with pasts. He had outcasts. I wonder how many of us choose not to be in the Christian community because of who already is in it.

What are the groups you are currently a part of? What does that group do to help you be a disciple of Christ? Do they know you and your gifts? Do they challenge you? Encourage you? Test you?

No Real Friends

I don't have time for friends.

I have friends but I don't really keep up with them.

Friendship is overrated.

My spouse is my only friend.

Friendship seems to have lost its value in the modern world. Americans report close friendships are at an all-time low. We are too busy and deep friendships take time. Being a friend requires sacrifice. By the time we are in our thirties, we often have a spouse, kids, a job, and a hundred other things pulling on our time. Who has the space for friends? When Jesus was in His thirties, He had twelve friends, or maybe only eleven.

Friendship is the natural outcome of being in any healthy community. If you participate in a healthy community, you will find your place, your gifting and inevitably a link with others who have common interests, common giftings, and common callings. These people will be your friends. They will walk with you, help you to grow and mature, share with you what they have learned and ask you what you have learned. You will laugh with them and cry with them.

The disciples vividly remembered that night at dinner. Jesus was in serious mode. He was teaching and telling them that soon He would be leaving them. Then He said, "I no longer call you servants . . . I now call you friends . . . I chose you" (John 15:15–16). He had entrusted to them everything He had learned from the Father. Jesus chose them to be His friends. Friendship is a core tenet of discipleship.

We all have the desire in us to be chosen as a friend. Can you imagine being picked out by God Himself to be a friend? Imagine that He delights in being with you and sharing His thoughts with you. Well, He does.

Who are your close friends? What behaviors led to this friendship? What keeps you from having more friends? What would you be willing to sacrifice to be friends? Do you believe God wants to count you as His friend?

Emotional Dysfunction

Nobody is trustworthy.

I have been hurt so many times I don't think I can take it again.

I am not worth loving.

No one has my best interest in mind.

Physical abuse, verbal abuse, sexual abuse, abandonment, betrayal, violence, false accusation, trauma, mockery, hatred, and rejection are all real. There is evil in the world, and we have been on the giving and receiving end.

There are volumes of books on emotional health, healing, and emotional IQ. It is helpful to read some of these, but let me boil it down to one simple truth: We have all been wounded and are in need of emotional healing. There is a core wounding that has a competing message with the gospel. There is a voice that speaks to us out of past pain that tries to influence every aspect of our lives.

The apostle Paul tells us that he does the very things he does not want to do and that he has a thorn in his flesh that never goes away. We will be tempted to believe the messages from our past pain instead of the truth of the gospel. Since we are all in this battle, we must fight the good fight.

We do not win this fight alone. We all need community. We need others to help us take these thoughts captive, to help us see our blindsides and weaknesses, and to walk with us through the pain into health and healing.

A mature disciple can tell you the most painful events of their life. They can explain the core wounding and competing messages with the gospel that came out of these experiences. They have had victories in these areas of their life and can identify those who helped them through these difficult times.

What is your core wounding? What competing beliefs do you have that are counter to the Gospel? What tapes play over and over in your head that keep you from sharing your heart with others? Who is helping you? What are your blind spots? What are you currently doing to seek emotional health?

Fear of Being Found Out

If anyone really knew me, they would be shocked

If people knew what I did, they would avoid me.

If I am found out, it's all over; my life is a fraud.

If I create a persona that people like, I will have friends.

Many successful businessmen, actors, and authors have admitted that they do not know what they are doing, that their life is a sham, and that they have a fear of being found out. An Academy Award winning actress, Kate Winslet, confided: "I'd wake up in the morning before going off to a shoot, and think, I can't do this; I'm a fraud."

Christians struggle with the same fear and shame because we never fully measure up to even our own expectations, much less those of the community around us. When we do get off track, it is hard to admit our failure to others, and we are tempted to put on an air of confidence and competence that we know is unfounded.

Once we leave out the part of the story that makes us look bad or shines a light on a real fault, we simply continue the sham and get deeper and deeper into the need to project our false self. We really believe the false self is safer than who we really are.

Now let me burst your bubble. People do see through our false personas. Those around us recognize the things that are off. We are not as good at hiding as we think we are. So, relax because our masks are not nearly as good as we think. Stop spending so much time trying to convince those around you that you have it all together and get busy finding people with whom you can be real and honest without judgment.

Christian community understands this and, in love and grace, helps us grow comfortable with who we are in front of others. We start to compare less. We start to reveal more of who we are. We recognize the gifts and weaknesses of others. We learn the strength of humility. We know we are not the savior, but we know who is.

Do you have fears of being found out? Do you think your life is a sham? Who knows you well enough to be open? Who speaks into your life and both encourages and challenges you? With whom can you shake your fears?

False Community

Entering college, I wanted to find a place to fit in and joined a fraternity. It was a place I could belong as long as I went along with all of its unhealthy behaviors. We had unspoken rules—do not confront anyone for drinking too much, sleeping around, or vandalizing other fraternities. These rules were not written down, but we all knew them and for the most part followed them.

So why do so many join false communities? If you are in a gang, you are more likely to be arrested, more likely to be murdered, more likely to be imprisoned, and more likely to be a victim of violence. So why do people join? Well, in the absence of other choices, we will choose an unhealthy community over no community. We choose gangs, cults, racist clubs, and immoral groups just to belong.

Paul was in a community of religious leaders called the Pharisees. He knew the rules, he played the game, and he became an important leader of that community. When the Christians showed up on the scene, he felt like they were a threat to his community and to his God. So, he went out and killed them.

When Paul became a Christian, he had people pray for him, love him, and help him identify his calling. Imagine the contrast! In his old club, he had to act like he had it all together. Now in the Christian community he could be himself.

What are the false communities you have been part of? What are the signs of false community? Where do you belong? What is expected of you to belong? What are the healthy communities you are a part of?

Want to explore community in greater depth? Please visit TheGood-Soil.us for a deeper discussion.

10

The Good Soil of Ministry

ONGOING CYCLE OF DISCIPLESHIP

IF YOU HAVE MADE it this far, congratulations! We are closing in on the end, so stay with me. Let us review. Calling comes first followed by equipping in the midst of community. This community will affirm our calling and gifting and give us direction as to what we should do with them—this is our ministry.

Billy Graham died recently. Here is what we know of him. He responded to the call of God to preach the gospel. He grew and matured. He honed his skills. He always worked with a team. He lived above reproach. He spoke to world leaders, and he affected the lives of millions, if not billions. His ministry was fruitful, and his life drew men, women, and children closer to God.

Before his death, Billy Graham, borrowing a thought from D. L. Moody whom he deeply respected, wrote this:

> Someday you will read or hear that Billy Graham is dead. Don't you believe a word of it. I shall be more alive than I am now. I will just have changed my address. I will have gone into the presence of God.[1]

This is a man who lived a life worth living. Certainly, he was not perfect, but somehow, he stayed above the fray. He lived out his calling and was equipped within the community. This led to an incredible ministry. I truly believe we all want to do the same. We want fruitful lives. Our ministry is what we do that bears lasting fruit. What is yours?

OLD TESTAMENT AND MINISTRY

In the Old Testament we see the symbolism of comparing Israel to a vine or a vineyard (Psalm 80: 8–15, Isaiah 5:1–7). The symbolism was to remind the Israelites that God has given them work to do. They were to care for the vineyard. Protect it from attack. Cultivate the soil. Prune the branches.

Moreover, since they have been blessed to be a blessing to others this caring for the vineyard should result in the production of fruit. Not fruit just for themselves but for others. For the poor, the outcast, and the stranger. The Israelites had a ministry, a ministry to hold up the Name of God. To live lives that gave God glory and that would draw others back to the One true God.

The prophets were sent to remind them they were failing in their ministry. They had forgotten their calling. They worked for themselves instead of for the Kingdom of God. They had forgotten their purpose. They were

---

1. "Someday You Will Read or Hear That Billy Graham Didn't Really Say That," Christianity Today, February 21, 2018, https://www.christianitytoday.com/ct/2018/february-web-only/billy-graham-viral-quote-on-death-not-his-d-l-moody.html

encouraged to return to the ministry of being God's chosen people so that all nations would know God.

JESUS AND HIS MINISTRY

When all the people were being baptized, Jesus was baptized too. And, as He was praying, heaven was opened, and the Holy Spirit descended on Him in bodily form like a dove. "And a voice came from heaven: 'This is my Son, whom I love; with him I am well pleased'" (Matthew 3:17).

Jesus' public ministry started at age thirty. He had been called by God, and His identity as God's Son was confirmed. Immediately after His calling, He was led by the Spirit into the desert. Here He went through equipping for forty days where He experienced and stood up to all that Satan could throw at Him. His character was challenged. He was told that God would not provide what He needed, God's authority was not sufficient, and that God's laws were made to be broken. Jesus' training in the desert opened the way for His ministry.

When He departed from the desert ready to begin His ministry, His first action was to form a community. He called His disciples together and illustrated that Christian life is done in community. It is then that His ministry to the people began.

Jesus did amazing things. He healed, He taught with authority, He developed leaders, He trained His disciples, He raised people from the dead, He prayed for those who rejected Him, and finally He died for those who sinned against Him.

When Jesus died on the cross, He said, "It is finished" (John 19:30). He had done all that He was called to do. He had been faithful and fruitful in His life and ministry. He had done what He set out to do. The effects of His ministry would endure. He had left nothing out. There were no gaps or regrets. His life on earth was complete, and He had finished well. Do we not all wish for this in our own lives?

JESUS AND HIS DISCIPLES

We clearly see that Jesus called His disciples, He equipped them in community, and then He sent them out to bear fruit. He expected them to be fruitful. Listen to the words He spoke to His disciples: "I chose you and appointed you so that you might go and bear fruit—fruit that will last" (John 15:16).

Disciples of Jesus develop an expectation that they will bear fruit. They will make a difference. They will participate in something bigger than themselves. They will affect and influence the lives of those around them. In short, they will have a ministry.

Jesus sends His disciples out to do ministry, and He has trained them so that He expects good things to happen. Disciples of Jesus can point to the good fruit in their lives. He also teaches them:

> You will know them by their fruits. Grapes are not gathered from thorn bushes, nor figs from thistles, are they? So, every good tree bears good fruit, but the bad tree bears bad fruit. A good tree cannot produce bad fruit, nor can a bad tree produce good fruit. Every tree that does not bear good fruit is cut down and thrown into the fire. So then, you will know them by their fruits. (Matthew 7:16–20 NASB)

Disciples of Jesus not only produce good fruit, but they can also distinguish good fruit from bad. Jesus wanted them to know that we all bear some kind of fruit in our lives, and it will either be good fruit that builds the Kingdom of God or bad fruit that pulls oneself and others away from God's Kingdom. Learn to tell the difference.

In the following passage, Jesus teaches us to expect good fruit from other disciples but to be patient.

> Then he told this parable: "A man had a fig tree growing in his vineyard, and he went to look for fruit on it but did not find any. So he said to the man who took care of the vineyard, 'For three years now I've been coming to look for fruit on this fig tree and haven't found any. Cut it down! Why should it use up the soil?' "'Sir,' the man replied, 'leave it alone for one more year, and I'll dig around it and fertilize it. If it bears fruit next year, fine! If not, then cut it down.'" (Luke 13: 6–9)

He gives them an image which illustrates that as they are patient for others to bear fruit, they can help create fertile soil so that fruitfulness may occur. We simply do not dismiss anyone that is unfruitful or bearing bad fruit. We fertilize, we dig around, and we do our part to help them be what they are created to be. But, at the end of the day, everyone is created to bear fruit.

The fig tree may have been beautiful and decorative, and offered pleasant shade in the summer. However, its primary purpose was to bear fruit; therefore, it was ultimately judged by what it produced and not by how it looked. Likewise, after we do all we can, if there is no fruit, we chop the tree down.

The disciples again were blown away one day when Jesus dropped this bombshell on them: "Very truly I tell you, whoever believes in me will do the works I have been doing, and they will do even greater things than these . . ." (John 14:12).

Jesus tells us that after He leaves this world, He will send us His Holy Spirit and that we will do greater things than He. Wow! He will empower us to do the things He is doing. Remember His plan is to use us, the church, this ragtag group, to change the world. If that is our task, we are going to need that kind of power and authority.

PAUL'S MINISTRY

We discussed Paul's calling earlier. He was then trained and equipped for three years in Arabia and probably another five to ten years in Tarsus before beginning his public ministry. His gifts and abilities were honed and assessed by the community. He was sent with a team to preach to the Gentiles, give advice on how to be the church, and raise up disciples who would continue the work.

Paul planted churches, preached the good news, endured persecution, and advanced the Kingdom of God. He wrote letters of encouragement, theology, and corrections that have become part of the Bible. He worked hard, and he bore much fruit.

In Ephesians 4:16, Paul explained to the disciples in Ephesus: "From him [Christ] the whole body, joined and held together by every supporting ligament, grows and builds itself up in love, as each part does its work." He was encouraging them that as they responded to the call of Christ, got clarity on their gifting, and formed a community, each part would do its work. All of humanity is wired for work. We desire to do something with our lives. We want to believe these promises and be a part of something greater than ourselves.

When Paul writes the disciples in Thessalonica listen to his words:

> For you yourselves know how you ought to follow our example. We were not idle when we were with you, nor did we eat anyone's

food without paying for it. On the contrary, we worked night and day, laboring and toiling so that we would not be a burden to any of you. We did this, not because we do not have the right to such help, but in order to offer ourselves as a model for you to imitate. For even when we were with you, we gave you this rule: "The one who is unwilling to work shall not eat." (2 Thessalonians: 3:7–10)

Idleness for Paul was not bad because of some random rule that everyone should work hard. He knew idleness would keep us away from the good work God has called us to do. When we choose to be idle, we are choosing not to respond to our calling.

TIMOTHY'S MINISTRY

Timothy grew up in a town called Lystra which was visited by the apostle Paul. Timothy began his training and equipping in his youth. The community recognized his calling, and Paul invited him on his missionary journey to Macedonia.

Timothy shared in the sufferings and joys of this journey. He heard Paul's teachings, observed, and participated in his way of life. He saw Paul live with faith, patience, and love. He witnessed Paul endure persecution and suffering. He learned to bear the fruit of ministry and help others bear good fruit. Paul leaves Timothy in Ephesus to lead the church. He commissions Timothy with these words:

> Timothy, my son, I am giving you this command in keeping with the prophecies once made about you, so that by recalling them you may fight the battle well . . .Be diligent in these matters; give yourself wholly to them, so that everyone may see your progress. Watch your life and doctrine closely. Persevere in them, because if you do, you will save both yourself and your hearers. (1 Timothy 1:18, 4:15–16)

Paul tells Timothy that he is ready to equip the disciples in Ephesus for all the good works God will call them to do.

WE ARE HERE FOR A REASON

When we wonder why am I here on earth? What is my purpose? What am I supposed to be doing? We are asking questions about ministry. Christianity provides an interesting and powerful answer to these questions.

First, we are to realize the desire of God is for all men to be saved (1 Timothy 2:4) and that he has made a plan to use us to partner with Him in this work. We are jars of clay who carry around the testimony and power of Christ Jesus so that God may be revealed (2 Corinthians 4: 7–11). We are his ragtag army outfitted with the truth of Jesus Christ called and equipped to go into the world and proclaim His name. We are his disciples and he has asked us to make disciples of all people in every nation. This work is our ministry.

Secondly, we are all to be a part of the effort. No one has been left behind to sit around and observe. We are not here simply to enjoy the view. We all are to put our hand to the plow. We are all invited to participate. The rich young ruler walked away from his invitation from Jesus (Matthew 19:22) and now we are to go find all those who have done likewise and invite them again. Jesus tells us the harvest is plentiful, but the laborers are few (Luke 10:2). We have work to do, and every person counts.

Finally, we work in a garden full of weeds. The ground is cursed and full of thorns and thistles (Genesis 3:17–18). The concerns of the world and wealth compete with the gospel of Jesus Christ. The world is a difficult place to do this work. We have to contend with suffering and evil in all our work. Ministry is a battle. Ministry is hard work. We will find rest in the end but not on this side of His return.

WE ARE TO BE FRUITFUL

I think as Christian's we struggle with Jesus when he says we will do greater things than he (John 14:12). It is hard to believe Jesus will empower us for great things. We think we do not deserve it. We think it is crazy to believe we will do greater things than God himself. We have a hard time believing we have been adopted as sons and daughter of the King and as God's children we are blessed to be a blessing to many. Fruit is the expected outcome of living the Christian life.

In Luke 13:6–9, Jesus tells us a parable about a tree that has not born fruit and the caretaker inquires if the tree should be destroyed. The caretaker knew the point of the olive tree was to bear more olives. In fact, the reality of gardening is that every vegetable has to bear fruit or become extinct. Bearing fruit is a part of nature. Bearing fruit is expected. Jesus is patient. He wants the caretaker to cultivate the soil first in an attempt to enable the tree to produce fruit in the next season. He then goes on to say that if there is no fruit next year, the tree should be cut down.

Jesus expects us to bear fruit. Sometimes we need some cultivation before we bear fruit, and He will be patient. He will put others in our lives to help us. But Jesus wants us to bear fruit, and there will come a time when He will inspect the fruit and make a decision as to whether or not to cut it down.

Yes, as disciples of Jesus, we are to bear much fruit. But take heart and remember that when we get clarity on our calling, humble ourselves for equipping, and are part of a healthy community, our ministry will become clear. We will not have gotten in front of God. We will not have skipped character development, healing, and training in righteousness. We will actually be prepared to do ministry. The soil in our lives has been cultivated, so we will not be surprised to see that we are actually bearing fruit in our ministry.

11

Working the Soil of Ministry

WHEN WE HAVE A ministry that comes out of a calling for which we have been equipped, and our calling has been affirmed by the community, we are eager to bear fruit. This chapter helps us understand how to work the soil of ministry.

I love to work in my garden. I plant the seeds, weed around the flowers and vegetables, and fertilize and water the plants. The growth and beauty following a season of planning and labor satisfies any soul. I partner with nature and God, see the beauty and fruitfulness, and enjoy the results. Gardening only makes sense if there is fruit as a result of one's effort.

Christians and, in fact, most of humankind intrinsically know that we have been created for a purpose, for work that yields results and is gratifying. People spend enormous amounts of time, energy, and resources to determine what kind of work they would be best suited for. They want to do work that has meaning and will make a difference in their lives and the lives of others.

We were created for relationship, but we were also created for work. This work for the Christian is your ministry. Everybody is called to ministry, called to expand the Kingdom of God. God gives all of us the call in the great commission to go into the world and make disciples. Yet He gives us distinct ministries within this larger call. (See 1 Corinthians12). Being faithful to our ministry builds on our calling and gifting and is done within the community. Our ministry should be discerned, evaluated, and guided on an ongoing basis.

Your ministry will line up with your calling. Use your gifting, and be affirmed and guided by the community. In your ministry you are called to bear fruit, not measured by worldly standards but by godly ones. This is often difficult to discern and easily confused in our consumer and numbers-driven culture. Wrong targets and analysis of success have led to many leaders forfeiting spiritual authority for the sake of worldly acclaim.

MINISTRY FLOWS OUT OF CALLING, EQUIPPING, AND COMMUNITY

I have a bad habit of getting out in front of God. I have not been accused of being overly patient. In my twenties, I got a sense that God was calling me to lead men's retreats. So, at the ripe age of twenty, I created my first retreat.

I did the research, planned the retreat, created flyers, and contacted everyone I knew asking them to sign up. The problem was that only one person signed up. So, I canceled. I was confused and frustrated. Had I not been called to this? Why would I be called and fail so miserably?

Fast forward twelve years. I was still not leading retreats. In fact, one day I was invited to go on a retreat just like the ones I had felt called to lead. I was angry at God, and I told Him. I asked why He would give me vision and not open the doors so I could participate in a fruitful ministry? Now I know: God planned this season of waiting on the vision because He was equipping me, building my character, and preparing me. I was not ready. He protected me from failures that I could not have recovered from.

Then the breakthrough came. I finally got the message that I was not to lead these retreats alone. Within a month, God brought a godly man into my life who had been undergoing a similar preparation. We shared our calling, we ran it by our communities, and we started retreats.

Now, I run many retreats a year as part of my calling. I have been prepared both in character and ability. I never lead them alone. To God's glory they bear much fruit.

Ministry comes out of our calling and equipping and in the context of Christian community. How often do we as Christians jump into ministry before the equipping, character building, healing, and team building processes?

Remember the Apostle Paul. He was certainly equipped intellectually. He had an elite mind and the ability to communicate hard truths in a way that others could understand. He was certainly called in an incredible fashion on the road to Damascus. But he still was not ready. He needed something like ten years to be prepared. Finally, one day Barnabas came knocking on his door. The time was ready for a missionary journey. Finally.

Jesus started His earthly ministry at the age of thirty. Do you think He was wasting His time? Sitting by idly? Or, perhaps He was being humble and taking on the limitations of man—subject to learning, training, and equipping.

Jesus created the same rhythms with His disciples. They were called, trained and equipped in both doing and being, their character issues were addressed, and then He sent them out.

Once we are called and equipped, we join a community, and the Lord gives us a ministry. He expects that His disciples will bear fruit. (See John 15:8.) He gives all of us the general call in The Great Commission to go into the world and make disciples. Yet, He gives us distinct ministries within this larger call. (See 1 Corinthians 12).

Being faithful to our ministry builds on our calling and gifting and is done within the context of community. Part of the community piece is the need for discernment, evaluation and guidance on an ongoing basis. Our Ministry will fit into the larger body of the one church and we will need this body to encourage, correct, and guide us.

When we have clarity on our calling and gifting and have received affirmation by the community with training, healing, and character development, our ministry will be satisfying to us and fruitful for others. When we skip any of these steps, our ministry is hampered, and we become frustrated disciples.

ACCOUNTABILITY

When I get off the rails, doing things I should not do or intentionally not doing the things I know are loving, I have a choice. I either spend time and energy trying to hide them from God and others or I bring them into the light. When I believe that I am in a safe, loving community, I usually choose to be accountable for my actions.

Conversely, I generally do not reveal these things to people I do not trust or to a group that would use it against me. Accountability is something we choose, and we usually choose it in healthy community. Accountability is not something "done" to us.

Every Friday, I meet with four men. It is a group of men who rarely express judgment, a group that fully embraces the gospel, a group that does not use information against one another. We encourage one another, we challenge one another, and we forgive and speak forgiveness to one another in the name of Jesus. I choose to be accountable to this group.

I have a friend who was an investigative journalist. He was tasked to infiltrate a local cult. At first, he thought they were kind and friendly, but there came a time when he was asked to reveal to them all of his darkest secrets and sins. They asked him about his sexual sins, criminal acts, and any sins he had kept hidden.

Knowing that all of these conversations were being recorded on a hidden camera and microphones, you can imagine his response—he lied. Even if it were not being filmed, he would have. He did not trust them. He knew it would be used against him down the road.

I think he made a good decision. Many people are not trustworthy enough to confess their darkest secrets. However, when we think no one is trustworthy enough, then we are choosing not to be accountable to anyone.

Accountability is a byproduct of healthy community. If we live as disciples in community, we will create a safe place where people can confess without judgment—a place where their sins are not used against them or as a source of shame, where they can be forgiven and restored, a place of hope despite the shortcomings. We all desire a community like this.

Accountability is often misunderstood by Christians. I often hear the phrase, "I am going to hold you accountable." You cannot make people accountable if they do not trust you. They will simply lie to or avoid you.

Jesus could not hold Judas accountable even though He knew his intentions (See Matthew 26:23). Jesus created the most fertile soil for Judas to choose accountability, and Judas opted out. Jesus did not hold the rich young ruler accountable; Jesus let him walk away (See Matthew 19:21–22).

Jesus was not interested in making people do right or in punishing them for their sins. This is what the Pharisees were good at. When they brought before Him a woman caught in the act of adultery, certainly something He should hold her accountable for, the Pharisees said to Jesus, "Teacher, this woman was caught in the act of adultery. In the Law Moses commanded us to stone such women. Now what do you say?" (John 8:4–5).

Jesus knew they wanted Him to affirm their policing of sin. He completely shocks them and turns the tables. Listen to His response, "Let any one of you who is without sin be the first to throw a stone at her . . ." (John 8: 7). He was saying judgment comes from those without sin—only God Himself.

Jesus was too wise for entrapment, so He followed this with a conversation with the woman:

"Has no one condemned you?"

"No one, sir," she said.

"Then neither do I condemn you," Jesus declared. "Go now and leave your life of sin" (John 8:10b–11).

Jesus was not going to police sin. He was going to lead people to repentance; there is a big difference. He did not condone her actions. He knew the way to the Lord was not through demanding rule following, but through deep repentance.

What kind of communities are we creating—ones you trust that will lead you to repentance or ones that police and encourage you to hide your sins?

To whom do you choose to be accountable? Where is the safe community that you trust? Friends? Family? Church? Small group? Have you experienced people trying to hold you accountable though they were not people you trusted? Have you done this to others?

SACRED SECULAR DIVIDE

I have many friends and family who, as they get older and their spouses develop serious health issues, have to prioritize their main ministry simply to caring for their loved one. "Let us not become weary in doing good, for at the proper time we will reap a harvest if we do not give up" (Galatians 6:9). They do not find themselves in the spotlight. They are not working in the four walls of the church Building. They are serving, cleaning, loving, and caring for people in ways no one will ever see.

Church work does not equal ministry. Let me say it again: church work does not equal ministry. In fact, the majority of ministry—the things the Lord calls you to do—are what is thought of as secular. This false dichotomy has done significant harm to discipleship in the West. Unfortunately, we think paid pastors do ministry and that ministers are the paid employees of the established church.

Everyone is ultimately called to a ministry. There are no exceptions. Ministry is both "secular and sacred." Ministry is an intentional response to what the Lord has done for you. Ministry is neither sacred nor secular but both at the same time. Your ministry will line up with your calling, work through your gifting, and be affirmed and guided by the church. In your ministry you will have fruit—not by worldly standards but godly ones. This is often difficult to discern and not confuse.

When I talk about ministry, I am not talking about church work. Certainly, much of the work done in the church is ministry, but ministry is much, much broader. We have a ministry to our family, a ministry to our spouse if we are married, a ministry to our children if we are parents, a ministry to those we work with, and a ministry to those in our neighborhood; and, all of that comes before we have church work.

When we look at the life of Jesus, both He and His disciples spent most of their time in "secular" settings. They were fishing, hanging out at the local watering hole, celebrating at parties, and only sometimes were they at a religious event or venue. Our ministry is often bringing the holy to unholy places.

COUNTING THE COST

Tim, a friend of mine, did something I often do. He acted before he counted the cost. There was a situation where a high-risk child was being removed from her family. Tim was currently mentoring the father, but the father was arrested and put in jail. The child had nowhere to go except foster care. Tim, out of love, offered to take her into his home.

After a while it became clear that the situation was untenable. His family simply was not equipped to do this work. They had no other small children in the house and their schedules and habits were not helping the child. She felt afraid and out of place. The child was not prospering. Tim finally realized he did not have the time and competency to serve her well. She was put into foster care.

I have often tried to go out to do great things for God with the thought that any good thing is worth doing. So, whenever I was doing something good, I reasoned that it must be ministry. The result of this process was that I faced all kinds of opposition and struggles I was unable to handle. Eventually my enthusiasm would wane, and in the end, I would give up. When I do not count the cost before committing to something, I end up doing the wrong things.

In Luke 14, a great crowd was following Jesus. He had been healing people, performing miracles, and teaching with great authority. (It must have been fun just to be around Him. I am sure it was tempting to join up just for the entertainment value.) As the crowd grew Jesus stopped and addressed them. He said, "Hey, y'all. If you are going to be my disciples, you better know what you're getting into; you'd better count the cost; you need to be ready to carry a cross and be prepared for a battle. And you will sacrifice everything to follow Me." (Luke 14:25–33, Author's Paraphrase.)

You can bet this thinned out the crowd a bit, but I imagine it also solidified something in the hearts of His disciples. Since they surely reflected on what the cost of discipleship was for them, when they chose to continue to follow Jesus, it was with a greater understanding.

When we create soil that allows people to become disciples without realizing what they are signing up for, the results are disastrous. We unintentionally form consumer Christians that avoid the difficult things. We create soil where discussing hard things like suffering is taboo. We create a soil where growth is severely stunted. We have done a disservice to many by focusing on all the benefits of our faith without having them count the cost of discipleship.

What are the costs of discipleship? How do you count those costs? What are you willing to sacrifice to be a disciple? What are the signs that one is a consumer Christian? What is needed in your life to improve this soil?

PLANNING

I made a plan to go to medical school without prayer or input from those who knew me best. When that plan did not work, I was tempted to think planning is overrated and unreliable. I was tempted to think plans are a waste of time because who can predict what will happen.

For this reason, planning has gotten a bad reputation recently. We get way ahead of God and plan things for our own success and glory. The plans contain little to no suffering. Of course, these plans ultimately fail.

The failure, however, is not in the planning itself. It is the process of planning that comes up short. If you are clear about the call and have been equipped for the ministry task and affirmed in that ministry by the community that this ministry is a fit, then it is time to plan.

"Surely the Sovereign Lord does nothing without revealing his plan to his servants . . ." (Amos 3:7). God's nature is to reveal, and He reveals His plans to His servants. God delights in revealing His plans so that His plans become our plans. Good plans lead to good fruit.

Scripture reveals that Christians who seek the Lord in their planning prosper: "Commit to the Lord whatever you do, and he will establish your plans" (Proverbs 16:3). This proverb assumes the importance of having a plan for our lives and that seeking the Lord will ensure it is a good plan. All effective ministry has these two components: it is of the Lord, and there is a plan.

A good friend of mine, David, is an amazingly gifted planner. When we have worked together on projects, he always reminds me that there is freedom in a good plan. I have always been a big proponent for just winging it. I call it being flexible or organic. Now with the help of David, I realize having a plan actually increases my freedom. Not having a plan increases my anxiety.

When I am living life with a plan that is in accordance with my calling, lines up with my gifting, and is affirmed by the community, there is immense freedom. I actually start enjoying life and ministry more. I notice there is not the gnawing voice repeating, "Am I doing the right thing or am I wasting my time?" What I thought was freedom or an "organic" process (no plans) was actually pushing me forward at a frantic pace that sucked the life out of me.

With a good plan, I have a filter for what to say yes to and, more importantly, what to say no to. I can set the course for a season. Of course, I make adjustments and tweak the plan, but I am not continually questioning the direction that I am taking. I can get off course, but now I am much quicker to realize that I am off course because I have clarity on where I am going.

It is also important that we do not fall in love with a plan and make the plan itself the thing to serve. We serve the Living God, and the plans we have are only good when they proceed from the Father. This helps focus our calling and results in fruitful behavior.

Good teachers have a teacher's plan, good leaders have a leadership plan, and good disciples have a discipleship plan. How do you go about planning? Is your planning a response to your calling and equipping and done in community? What is the plan you are currently working on? Who helps you plan?

GOALS AND EVALUATION

I ask a lot of people at the end of the year the following question, "How did you do?"

They are confused and say, "What do you mean?"

I say, "How did you do this year? Did you accomplish what you thought you would? What was the fruit? Where did you fall short? How will that inform what you do next year?"

The most common reply: "Good questions. I don't know. I have not really thought about it that much. I don't know if I reached my goals because I did not set any goals."

Good planning always leads to goal creation and evaluation. When we have goals, we take time to stop and see if we are on the right track. Anything worth doing is worth evaluating. It is natural for most of us to have questions when we are doing something important: Am I doing this right? Am I on the right track? What should I do next? Am I going to be successful? What should I be doing differently?

A key to discipleship is to take that natural tendency and enter into healthy processes of goal setting and evaluation. The enemy is happy to have you doing ministry that is a burden to you and ineffective for the community. Evaluation is crucial to joy-filled Kingdom work.

Many of us do not even know what fruit our ministry is supposed to produce. We do not know how to describe the fruitfulness of our lives. We may even think that it is prideful to talk about the fruit of our lives. Remember in 2 Corinthians 11, Paul actually boasts about his sufferings.

When our identity is established in our calling as sons and daughters of God and we have been equipped, we do not avoid evaluation. We welcome it. Evaluation is not an attack on our identity; it is not something that makes us feel like failures; it is a humble and appropriate response to the promises of the Lord.

We welcome God and the community to come around us because we are secure. The heart of Romans 8 is that no outside failure could derail us as disciples because we are already victors. The Psalmist asks of God, "Point out anything in me that offends you, and lead me along the path of everlasting life" (Psalm 139:24 NLT).

We want our ministry to be successful so when we struggle, we turn to Him and the body of Christ for aid and direction and discernment. If we know that we have been called and equipped in both being and doing, and the community affirms our ministry, we welcome input and feedback. In fact, healthy disciples seek and create time and occasions to be evaluated by others.

In your ministry what are your goals? How will you know you have achieved them? Who is helping you evaluate? How often do you set goals and evaluate them?

TWO BY TWO

There are many things in the Bible that seems unclear or vague. Jesus' desire for our doing ministry two by two is not one of them. He always sent His disciples out two by two. Even when He just needed a donkey to ride, yes, you guessed it—He sent two disciples.

Jesus' model was impressed on the disciples, and the early church continued with this policy. Every missionary journey had at least two disciples. They knew the power in community. They knew ministry done alone is subject to failure at much higher rates.

Your ministry needs to be with others. When you have an individual ministry, your blind spots become huge dangers. When you do ministry with others you not only help each other see each other's blind spots you also bring varying strengths and gifts. I believe the practice in our church of letting individuals do ministry alone is the most dangerous habit the church has silently endorsed.

When we hear about someone who has been taken out with drugs, affairs, or greed, more than likely they are doing life alone. When we look at the pastors who have famously fallen, we notice that they were not partnered with another disciple. They were in it alone. When we struggle and sin, most of the time, we are by ourselves.

When we are willing to work with others there is built in accountability. There is built in encouragement. There are built in places to process ideas. It leads to more prayer. It models the Trinity.

Who are you partnered with? What are the things you try to do alone? What part of the Body are you and what is the complementary part that would make your ministry complete?

YELLOW FLAGS OF MINISTRY

As we embark on the ministry we are called to do and work on the habits mentioned in this chapter. Let's look at some of the key warning signs and yellow flags that will help us in our ministry pursuits. Recognizing these early will save you and your community from lots of frustration.

NO PLANS OR GOALS

"I don't make plans; they just box me in."

"Why make plans? Everything just changes and you always have to rework them."

"I don't have any goals for myself."

"Goals are not Christian; they are expressions of our corporate culture."

When you are learning a new game or sport one of the first things you want to know is how do you score? Then how do you win? What is the objective? When do you know when it's over? Try to imagine a game or sport where there is no scoring, no winner, no object to achieve or purpose, and it never ends. No one would want to play.

How about a life with no goals, no purpose, no way to know if you have had any success or achievements, no objectives, and no end—I am pretty sure I just described Hell!

Why would disciples of the Lord be content with a life void of purpose? Plans and goals are the infrastructure of a life with purpose. They flow out of God's call on our lives.

UNHEALTHY EVALUATION

"Why do I need to be evaluated?"

"Evaluations are just ways to manipulate others."

"Evaluations only focus on what is wrong with me and they just bring me down."

"When I get called in to the boss's office, I know something is up, that I have done something wrong."

I get it. As Christians we are not doing a great job of evaluating our lives as disciples. We have used evaluations to hurt people or manipulate situations.

We have done evaluations in place of having the hard, loving conversations we need to have with one another.

I once had a boss who could not keep employees for any length of time. I spoke to most of the staff when they left. The one common theme about why they left was the way they were being evaluated. They felt put down, underappreciated, and even verbally abused when they were being evaluated.

The abuse of evaluation has led many disciples to avoid them altogether. Fear of evaluation is on the rise because it has been done so poorly. Consequently, as disciples of Christ we don't know what should be evaluated, how often or through which lenses.

Unhealthy evaluation falls into two camps. First, there are those who do not evaluate because they do not want to hurt people's feelings or deal with tough issues. Because of this fear, many organizations do not know how to evaluate; and, I get asked to come in to evaluate for them.

I was asked to conduct a holistic evaluation of a church leader up for promotion. Let's call him Ben. Ben fought me the whole way. Ben was offended that others had anything negative to say about him and rejected all of their feedback as an expression of their own faults.

What became clear in this process was that Ben could not identify his own weaknesses. Ben never laughed at himself, he took himself too seriously, and he never received feedback from others. He avoided conflict at all costs. When criticized, he responded with slander. Before I finished my report, he was hired. The report sits on my computer unread.

Within a year Ben created a coup d'état and formed his own organization where he could be in charge and could avoid further evaluation. He caused severe relational and financial hardship on many.

Another way disciples have been exposed to unhealthy evaluation comes from evaluation based only on the surface or outward appearance. When I work with churches, I ask them what gets evaluated the most. Their response is always "money and numbers."

I agree and tell them three things:

1. Those are evaluated the most because they are easy to count.

2. Those are counted because they do tell you something; they are important.

3. There is something more important to evaluate that reveals the depth of discipleship. But it is harder to evaluate, so it gets ignored.

We just are not good at figuring out how to evaluate those things. Nevertheless, we must try because it is possible. This book hopes to bring to the surface many of the things that are worth evaluating but are often overlooked. Let us get creative in figuring out how to evaluate the aspects of discipleship that are so critical to the ongoing maturing of our faith.

With few exceptions, pastors tell me they are good preachers. When I probe, I find that they all base their preaching ability on the same standard. They tell me that when they preach others tell them after the service how meaningful or good it was.

Rarely ever do they have an effective tool to evaluate their preaching. Maybe they are good, but they do not ask if their message is too short or too long or if it is good for newcomers or for those who have been discipled for years or both. One or two comments after a service is sufficient for them. I encourage them to press in because:

They do not know if they rely only on right brain communication. Are they able to give listeners visual images to make points stick?

They do not know if their ability to tell stories needs work or if they have a tendency to repeat themselves—they do not know because they never ask the questions.

I find the tendency to avoid evaluation to be even more true for those who do not get praised or honored to do their ministry. It is as if they are doing their ministry as a favor to God and no one has the right to evaluate what they are doing. After all, they are just doing it out of the goodness of their heart. Who would be so cruel and ruthless as to comment on their work?

If I am volunteering to read a scripture at a service and I do not prepare and do a poor job, should I be evaluated? If I am handing out food at a food bank and my attitude is a bit surly, should I be evaluated?

Jesus tells us that we will know true disciples by their fruit. The ones who use their talents and bear fruit will be rewarded and the ones who bury them in fear get weeping and gnashing of teeth (See Matthew 25:14–30).

How do you know if you are being fruitful? What are you evaluating? Have you been evaluated in unhealthy ways? Do you avoid evaluation?

IDENTITY TIED TO EVALUATION

"I am only as good as my last success."

"If I don't think I'll be successful, I avoid it."

"I am important; look at what I have done."

"The approval of others keeps me going."

145

I still remember my first "F" in school. It was a spelling test and I only got one word right. I had studied and thought I had done well. As a child it was devastating. I did not want my parents to see my grade and feared that classmates might see it. This failure, I thought made me a failure.

I still cannot spell. Thank God for spell check. Whenever I write I misspell LOTS of words. When I write on the whiteboard in meetings, I misspell words. This is a weakness of mine that will not go away. However, now as a child of God, I know my identity is not tied to my outward failures. So, I have no problem asking for help when I have to write.

Your identity as God's son or daughter is the fertile soil for evaluation. When every evaluation is perceived as an *ad hominem* attack or slight on you or your character, your identity in Christ is not fully formed. When you hear correction and immediately defend yourself, you are not open to correction; you think it is an attack on your personhood.

We do not know how to evaluate the deeper things that we believe are vital. Most people do not really want the deep evaluation that should be normative for a Christian disciple. We believe protecting our identity or our reputation outweighs what we might learn from any evaluation. We do not trust the systems because we see them as an existential threat to our being.

Why do we love compliments? Why do we need affirmation? Why do we desire approval? Because we have a built-in need to be fruitful, and the compliment, affirmation and approval are signs that we are doing something worthy of praise, that we are being productive, that we are doing something worth doing.

But when the compliments, affirmation, and identity come from the things we do instead of from our Father in heaven we are in danger. We will order our lives around the people and situations that give us praise and conversely, we will avoid and flee from anything that reveals our faults, weakness, or sin. This is a very destructive place to be as a Christian. We are perfected only by our identity being established by the atonement of the cross.

Are you secure in your identity? Are you rocked by evaluations? Negative feedback? Outward failures? Do you seek out or rely on compliments and/or awards?

FEAR OF FAILURE

"I already know I can't do it."

"I can't handle anymore criticism."

"If this doesn't work, I don't know what I will do."

"Nothing I do ever works out."

Many leadership books explain that the way to really grow is to fail and to learn from those mistakes. Despite all the advice to "fail forward" and to see your failures as opportunities to grow, the fear of failure looms over the Christian community. Certainly, this may come from the community being overly harsh or judgmental, but more often it is a core message that resides in the hearts of many—a message that says failure is not part of the Christian life.

I have spoken to many followers of Christ who confess that the fear of failing—of coming up short, or disappointing others—paralyzes them. They are literally prevented from taking action by such fears. This, I am afraid, is nothing new. When Jesus was training His disciples, He told them, "I say to you, My friends, do not be afraid of those who kill the body and after that have no more that they can do" (Luke 12:4 NASB).

Jesus knew fear has the power to both motivate and paralyze. Fear can drive us to ill-advised action or deter us from wise action. Disciples have to learn what to fear and what not to fear. When we fear the Lord, unhealthy fears lose their power over us. As Christians we know God "gave us a spirit not of fear but of power and love and self-control" (2 Timothy 1:7 ESV). I am sure the Apostle Paul figured out going on missionary journeys was going to involve rejection, failure, and suffering; He just learned not to fear those moments and was able to have the posture that "we are hard pressed on every side, but not crushed; perplexed, but not in despair; persecuted, but not abandoned; struck down, but not destroyed" (2 Corinthians 4:8–9).

What do you fear? What keeps you from your ministry? What do you do out of fear that drains you? How do you recognize fear in your life? Can you see when other Christians are living in fear?

AVOID CONFLICT

"A fight is not worth the energy."

"I don't want to lose this relationship over a fight."

"I can't handle the stress of more conflict."

"Sometimes I think it's better to just walk away."

I finally figured out the economy of conflict. The more I avoid conflict, the more stressed I am, and the longer it takes to move forward. I don't know why this realization took me so long. Most of my early life I developed plans and strategies to avoid conflict. I saw conflict as a net loss game.

In some communities there is a culture where Christians are expected to avoid conflict. Christians are supposed to be "nice." Christians should never have to have hard conversations. We are told Jesus was meek and mild and if we want to be like Jesus, we should do everything in our power to get along with everyone regardless the cost. We are not supposed to rock the boat. Conflict means someone is wrong and good Christians should never have anything go wrong.

We forget Jesus rebuked His best friend, drove out the money changers with a whip He made, and stood up to the powerful religious leaders and corrupt government officials. It is safe to say He did not avoid conflict so that everyone would think He was nice.

Jesus sent His disciples out knowing they would face conflict. The early church sent missionaries out knowing this would cause conflict. Paul, Barnabas, Timothy, and John Mark certainly dealt with conflict on a regular basis. Today you can be sure whatever your ministry is, it will involve conflict.

How do you deal with conflict? Are you overly passive or aggressive in conflict? Do you catch yourself hoping things will just work themselves out? Did you have bad experiences with conflict in your family or workplace that still affect you? How can you learn to deal with conflict in a Christian way?

UNCLEAR BATTLE PLAN

> "Today you are going into battle against your enemies. Do not be
> fainthearted or afraid; do not panic or be terrified by them. For
> the Lord your God is the one who goes with you to fight for you
> against your enemies to give you victory" (Deuteronomy 20:3b–4).

When you try to live out your ministry there will be resistance. This is normal. This is predictable, and yet many seem to think that if they are doing their ministry the right way, nothing should get in the way. Actually, it is the complete reverse. There is an enemy and he will fight over any ministry we are involved in that will draw people to God.

When we lose focus on who is the enemy and whom we are fighting we neglect an important part of our ministry. When we think our ministry will always work out without resistance, we get negligent in our preparation.

Too many times, I have stepped into ministry without developing a clear plan. This oversight certainly put me at a disadvantage on the battlefield. I learned the hard way. Now I am more intentional to clearly identify the enemy and his strategies for assaulting the ministry I am involved in. The better we get at this the less our ministries suffer.

Jesus faced this resistance throughout His ministry. The enemy was working to kill, destroy, and mock everything He was doing. It never stopped. Even on the cross Jesus was mocked and insulted by one of the criminals: "Aren't you the Messiah? Save yourself and us!" (Luke 23:39). And, when they nailed Jesus to the cross, His response to His tormentors was, "Father, forgive them for they don't know not what they do" (Luke 23:34).

Jesus knew the enemy was Satan—not the people who were simply his mouthpiece or unwitting servants. That is why we can love our enemies and bless those who curse us. We can understand the battle, we can know who the enemy is, and we can have a plan for victory.

Do you see your ministry as a battle? Against what or whom? What is your current battle plan? Who else is in your platoon fighting the same battle?

OVER-PACKED SCHEDULE

"How can I do more than I'm already doing?"

"I'm swamped. I'll get to that when I have more time."

"I can't afford to take a vacation. There is just too much that has to get done."

We have convinced ourselves that if we stay busy, we are better off than the guy playing games on his computer at work. He is a goof-off and I am a hard worker. We stay busy so we can reason that we are working as hard as we can; so, if there is no fruit in my life, it cannot be my fault. I am doing everything I can. We stay busy to justify why we are not doing the hard work of discipleship.

We are all involved in this modern attack on our schedules. We go, go, go. We have little, if any, margins in our lives. We brag to others that our calendars are full. We believe the lie that if we are busy all the time there is nothing more we can do. We justify our lives with the excuse that we have no more time to do anything else. Consequently, we think we have no more room in our lives for deep discipleship.

Brian Regan is one of my favorite comedians. He points out that if you find yourself microwaving a Pop-Tart for 15 seconds instead of toasting it for a minute to save time, you might want to loosen your schedule up a bit. Christians need margins in their lives. Imagine this page in this book if there were no margins at the top, sides and middle. What if there were no margins between paragraphs or words? We certainly could get more words on each page, but it would be a disaster. It would take forever to understand what I was writing. Margins add value, give meaning, and are necessary part of our lives.

Jesus was always in demand. He could have worked day and night nonstop. He could have justified the work because there were plenty of sick people to be healed and plenty of outcasts who needed to be invited in. And there was plenty of wisdom to be dispensed to His disciples before He left them in charge. His disciples before He left them in charge. Yet, we see that He was never in a hurry. He did not rush. In fact, He regularly got away just to be with His Father.

One day, one of Jesus' followers pleaded with Him to rush to their house because their brother Lazarus was desperately sick and needed Him. Jesus responded by tarrying for a few days before going to see His friend.

When He arrived, Lazarus was dead. Mary told Jesus that if He had been there sooner, Lazarus would not have died.

Can you imagine what would have happened if Jesus had dropped everything and rushed to the aid of Lazarus? We would be using that as a model to justify our crazy pace of life. Jesus knew His ministry was perfected, not because of how much He did or how fast He did it, but rather because it was grounded in the will of the Father. Jesus raised Lazarus from the dead and explained that the purpose of the whole episode was to give glory to the Father.

How tight is your schedule? Do you have the margins to do the things God asks of you? What are your habits for taking time off? Are you exhausted when you start your vacation? Do you realize that your schedule actually may be hindering you from doing your ministry?

COASTING

"I just go with the flow"

"It pays the bills, but I hate my job."

"I'm just going through the motions"

"I can't wait until retirement."

Certainly, there are times where we are meant for rest, for being, and for sabbatical. There are also times for clarifying calling and getting equipped, but we always have a question for the Lord as to what specifically we should be doing. What is my current ministry? If you go for a long time without clarity on your ministry you languish, you get frustrated, you lose your sense of purpose, and you view retirement as a season where you are not responsible to do ministry. These are soul-killing thoughts.

If you do not know your current ministry, you are in danger. Broadly speaking you will always have a ministry to your family, your spouse, your children, and your friends. There may be times where it is that simple. My mom is in her 70's and, unfortunately, her husband (my stepfather) has developed Alzheimer's. It is a terrible disease, and right now it is fair to say her whole ministry is the care of her husband. This is the deepest of ministries which demands humble sacrifice. The world is watching the way we minister to the least of these.

You will always have a ministry, you never are finished, and you never get to coast on some past work. You are created to do the things God has prepared for you and there will always be those things, whether you have a job or are retired, whether you are sick or healthy, and whether you want to or not. A healthy Christian community will help you see your ministry in every stage of your life and help you develop as a disciple.

When I go through a long hard season of ministry I do yearn for downtime. I want and need a break. But when I start to view the break as the goal or my preferred state, I get in trouble. I can start to resent ministry. I can believe the lie that my life is much more enjoyable if I stay away from the hard work of ministry. I have been there and do not want to go back.

How do you view vacation and or time off? Is it the reward of ministry? How long is healthy to take a break from ministry? What rhythms do we see in the life of Jesus on this topic?

REACTING VS INITIATING

"There is always a pressing need"

"The circumstances are beyond my control."

"I am powerless to do anything."

"I quietly accept who I am."

Friedman, in his book, *A Failure of Nerve* explains the consequences of feeling stressed and/or attacked. When we feel this way, we have a natural tendency to rely on our reptilian brain. We respond without thinking. We purely react to the outside circumstances. We devolve into the primitive fight or flight instinct. In short, we simply react to everything.

While this instinct works well for us when we are in truly dangerous situations it becomes debilitating to function well in the everyday world. But increasingly, in our culture, people report higher levels of stress and see others as more of a threat. The result is that we become more reactive and take less initiative.

Initiative is the fuel of ministry. Ministry cannot be simply reacting to everything around us. When we sense the call of God for a ministry, it is initiative that gets us in position to do the work. Too many times in my ministry I look up and realize days have gone by and I have spent most of my time and energy reacting to the things around me. To problems. To complaints. To things that did not go as planned. I have to stop and reorient myself back to the calling. I have to take initiative to step into the promises of God and depower my interpretation of my circumstances.

When you think about emails, is your job primarily about answering them or creating them. If email for you is primarily about answering someone else's questions, you may be living a reactive life versus an initiating life. When we let others dictate our agenda, schedule, or focus, we will soon lose sight of our true ministry.

Way too many of us order our lives in reaction to the needs and circumstances around us. We think our ministry is to put out all the fires that are started in our lives and in the lives of those around us. At first it feels good; we are doing something; we are doing something helpful; we are doing something that is helping; and we reason that this must be good, this must be my ministry. I am good because all the things I am doing are good things. This has trapped and derailed more Christians than you can imagine; but in reality, this is a cop out. We can avoid seeking the Lord for our true calling, We can avoid the equipping we need because we are so busy. We can avoid being in a healthy community that helps us discern our true ministry.

What puts you in a reactive mode? What motivates you to take initiative? When do you get stuck in a cycle of responding to everything around you? Did Jesus take initiative or react in His ministry?

LONE RANGER MINISTRY / LONE RANGER LIFE

"I can do it on my own—I don't need anyone."

"If you want it done right, do it yourself."

"I don't trust anyone—no one can do it as well."

"It's easier if I just do it myself."

Many stories in American culture are stories of individuals who did great things. We love the Supermen! We idolized the self-made man. We are tempted to think that if we need others, it makes us weak. We like to believe we have everything in us that we need to make it on our own.

Here is what I thought about others in ministry: There are more problems when we deal with others. Others get in the way of progress. Everyone does not do it the way I think they should. The more people the more complicated things get. I cannot control others. Others do and say things that hurt me. It will be easier to do it by myself.

After many years of doing ministry in most part all on my own I felt empty and alone. Here is the problem with all thing things listed above, they were true—it is hard working with others. But it was not the whole truth and partial truths always come back to bite us.

I could not forget the biblical mandate that we are to be part of the body. I could not dismiss the fact that I did not have all the gifts needed for the ministry I was in. I knew I needed others. I took steps to do ministry with others. Let me share with you some valuable lessons I have learned that are also true. I am better off with others. I need the gifts of others to have success in ministry. It is more fun with others. Ministry is more effective when does as a team. Trying to get credit for things is empty and exhausting. Sharing victories with others is joyous.

We have all worked with others who have made the job harder or even ruined the project. We all have been tempted to respond by going it alone. We have been hurt and frustrated by others' actions. We have isolated ourselves in response. I encourage you to press on doing ministry with others because there is much more at work.

I realized a failed ministry was often part of God's plan. He used others to show me the pride I possessed. He used others to grow my character. He used others to help me identify with His suffering. It was not so much getting the job done as it was developing in me a humility that comes from working with others.

Humility admits that I do not have all the gifts and I actually need others. Humility admits that I have blind spots that others can help me with. Humility admits that God created me to be in relationship with others. Humility recognizes all good things come from God. Humility knows we are limited human beings.

What is your ministry and who do you share it with? What part of the body are you? How might God be using others in your life and ministry to develop humility? What might the Lord be asking you to add, change or remove from your ministry?

Want to explore issues around your Ministry? Go to TheGoodSoil.us for more discussion.

12

Conclusion and Final Thoughts

TO INDIVIDUALS

First, let me say congrats for pushing through and finishing the book! I hope it helps cultivate the soil of your discipleship. I hope that it gave you a broader imagination for a robust Christian discipleship plan for life. I hope you are aware that there is so much more for you as a Christian— that now you not only have some answers, but, more importantly, you have better questions.

I know you have had an earnest desire to fully commit your life to the Lord but like so many others you have hit some roadblocks. I hope this book has shown you a way around or over them. I hope you can now identify the things you need to add to the soil and are better equipped to see the yellow flags that adversely affect the soil.

I encourage you to ask yourself where you are in this season of discipleship:

1. Are you in a season to clarify calling?

2. Are you in a season where you need more equipping? Character development? Healing?

3. Are you in a life-giving community that helps you grow as a disciple?

4. What is your ministry? And, is it as fruitful as you hoped?

For the new Christian, your initial calling is fresh in your mind and often described in your story of conversion. Celebrate God's calling you, share your story with others, and know He continues to call you. Commit to a life of learning to listen to Him and to develop regular habits and rhythms of growth and maturing. Join a church community so you can process all that the Lord has put in your heart and mind.

For the reader who has been a Christian for a while, my intent has been to give you some idea of how to revisit your past calling and gain clarity on how your Father in heaven is speaking to you today so you can be more intentional about the equipping you need. Finally, I hope that you are in a ministry that is bearing much fruit!

Wherever you are in your journey, I hope you understand that the norm for the Christian should be a commitment to a lifetime of learning and growth. We need to recognize that God has been at work in our lives, is at work in our lives, and will always be at work in our lives.

If you did not have the time to visit the website TheGoodSoil.us while you were reading, I invite you into The Good Soil Community. Consider watching at least one of the videos or listen to a podcast to see if it spurs you on to a deeper understanding and expression of discipleship. Finally, if this book spoke to you, give it to a friend or to your pastor. Set up a time to discuss it and prayerfully consider the "All Church Challenge" described below.

TO CHURCHES AND OTHER CHRISTIAN ORGANIZATIONS

I would like to invite all pastors to participate in the "All Church Challenge." Buy a book for each family in your congregation or split the cost with them. Give everyone a month to read the book and jot down thoughts and questions.

Then have a few gatherings to discuss your discipleship platform. What are you doing well? What is missing? What needs to be tweaked? What areas need some outside help?

If you find this process does not help your church move forward in a significant way, we will buy your books back.[1]

What are you doing to create fertile soil for your people? What are you doing to make sure they are living into their calling and not laboring in vain? What are the structures you have set up to ensure your people are being discipled?

---

1. To qualify for this program, sign up on TheGoodSoil.us.

If we are not serving our people well in terms of equipping them for ministry, we run the risk of using people for our own agendas, treating them like cogs in a machine. We need to see them as *imago dei* not in terms of how they can help our church or organization accomplish tasks. This experience in my estimation is far too common in the modern church.

Once people are called, they need to revisit their calling, go deeper in their understanding of calling, and make the adjustments God is leading them to make. Evangelism is not enough. We must continue to help our people hear from the Lord on a regular basis as to what He would have them do.

Next, we must have a way to equip people both in terms of being and doing. What are you doing to equip them to live as Christians in the 21st century? How are they being taught to deal with an increasingly secular culture?

Are you just running program after program hoping it is working? Do you feel like your job is simply to keep things running smoothly? Or, are you ready to invite your community into a holistic approach to discipleship that challenges everyone in your congregation to grow and mature?

If you are an organization, you probably have only one or two areas of discipleship you are trying to bolster. Maybe you offer a tool of discipleship that helps the church, or you offer outside help or experiences that aid in discipleship. I encourage you to get clear on your part and how that fits into the whole. How you are helping the church and its pastor equip the saints for ministry?

If I can be of any help, please go to the website and contact me with your questions or request!

Blessings,
Allen Hughes

CPSIA information can be obtained
at www.ICGtesting.com
Printed in the USA
FSHW020204060521